FISH
of
ALBERTA

Joynt • Sullivan

Illustrations by Ian Sheldon

Lone Pine Publishing

© 2003 by Lone Pine Publishing
First printed in 2003 10 9 8 7 6 5 4 3 2
Printed in China

All rights reserved. No part of this work covered by the copyrights hereon may be reproduced or used in any form or by any means—graphic, electronic or mechanical—without the prior written permission of the publisher, except for reviewers, who may quote brief passages. Any request for photocopying, recording, taping or storage on information retrieval systems of any part of this work shall be directed in writing to the publisher.

The Publisher: Lone Pine Publishing
10145 – 81 Avenue
Edmonton, AB T6E 1W9
Canada
Website: http://www.lonepinepublishing.com

National Library of Canada Cataloguing in Publication Data

Joynt, Amanda, (date)
 Fish of Alberta / Amanda Joynt and Michael G. Sullivan.

 Includes bibliographical references and index.
 ISBN 13: 978-1-55105-191-8
 ISBN 10: 1-55105-191-5

 1. Fishes—Alberta. 2. Fishes—Alberta—Identification. I. Sullivan, Michael G. (Michael Gary), 1958– II. Title.
 QL626.5.A4J69 2003   597.176'097123   C2003-910234-3

Editorial Director: Nancy Foulds
Project Editor: Genevieve Boyer
Editorial: Genevieve Boyer
Technical Review: Mark Steinhilber
Production Manager: Gene Longson
Layout & Production: Elliot Engley, Lynett McKell
Book Design: Elliot Engley
Cover Design: Gerry Dotto
Cover Illustration: Bull Trout, by Ian Sheldon
Illustrations: Ian Sheldon
Maps: Lynett McKell, Elliot Engley
Separations & Film: Elite Lithographers Co., Edmonton, Alberta

Photography Credits
The photographs in this book are reproduced with the generous permission of their copyright holders. Craig Johnson, p. 4, 30, 31 & 34; Claudine B. Nelson, p. 5; Ian Sheldon, p. 10, 20, 22a, 22b, 24a, 24b & 25b; Linda Kershaw: p. 23a & 25a; Tamara Eder, p. 23b; Alan Bibby, p. 33; Amanda Joynt, p. 176a; Bill Patterson, p. 176b.

We acknowledge the financial support of the Government of Canada through the Book Publishing Industry Development Program (BPIDP) for our publishing activities.

PC: P15

CONTENTS

ACKNOWLEDGEMENTS

Thanks and gratitude go to the following people for their help in the writing of this book. Mark Steinhilber from the Provincial Museum of Alberta contributed loads of helpful technical advice. His hard work on this book is greatly appreciated. Joe Nelson deserves a big thank you for introducing Albertans to our fish species, as well as for his support of this book. Thanks to Wayne Roberts, Terry Clayton and Jim Stelfox for their suggestions and knowledge. This book would not have been possible unless the wonderful staff at Lone Pine had not put their heads behind it. Thanks especially to Genevieve Boyer, Nancy Foulds, Shane Kennedy, Elliot Engley, Lynett McKell, Gerry Dotto and Gene Longson. Ian Sheldon provided us with illustrations that went beyond what we had wished for—thank you for your patience and attention to detail. As well, this book is in memory of Dr. Martin J. Paetz, one of Alberta's first fisheries managers and a lifelong friend of Alberta's fishes.

A researcher holding Alberta's provincial fish, the Bull Trout.

FOREWORD

This book, rich in colour illustrations, is an enjoyable introduction to the many species of fish in Alberta. People of all ages, experiences and expectations will find this book a fun way to learn about Alberta's fish. It is an adventure in learning for avid anglers, those seeking to challenge themselves in fishwatching or for those just wanting to know what is in our midst.

Many people that I talk with, upon learning my profession, ask "What is an ichthyologist doing in Alberta?" There are many reasons—but one of them, as you are about to discover in this book, is that Alberta has a lot of fascinating fishes! Do you know how many species of fish are in Alberta? Fishwise, we are not in a completely barren wasteland. Yes, we are at or near the source of many Canadian rivers, generally not a good place for most fish. Yes, Alberta was recently glaciated. Yes, Alberta has less water than adjacent provinces. And yes, Alberta has a cold climate with our waters frozen for much of the year. If we are in a tough area for fish, then the fish we have are survivors. Readers will be surprised, I think, to discover the diversity of species that we do have in our province—and our fish species are so downright interesting. Do you know what species in Alberta is said to have venomous spines or what species has individuals that are sometimes called "Pinocchios"?

Identification of Alberta's fish species is emphasized in the book, and rightfully so. Do you already know how to identify more than 10—are you certain? There is much information on each species in this book, such as on their general biology, feeding and spawning. Do you know what part of which species was used historically to make wine, beer and jellies? Viewing tips will help readers not already into fishwatching see the diversity of species. We have some of the most primitive living freshwater fish species and some of the most derived. There is also much variation within each species of fish—more so than within species of birds and mammals—for example, in colour variation and variation in growth rates. Do you know that a fish never stops growing?

Authors Amanda Joynt and Michael Sullivan are to be congratulated for providing such a fine overview of Alberta's fishes. I am well acquainted with Michael, a highly innovative provincial biologist who is gaining recognition for his approach to fish management. Michael is very talented at convincingly explaining to the enlightened public just how good scientific practice leads to sound regulations in managing our fishes. He and his colleagues are truly dedicated in the face of many principal obstacles to ensuring fish populations in Alberta survive for future generations to enjoy.

Our fishes deserve our attention, and dare I say they deserve our care and love. We can watch them and get to know them on a first-name basis. It is by knowing the fishes, whether through angling, watching or just knowing that they are there, that we can receive enjoyment and at the same time be on watch for their long-term survival. It is a pleasure to see that fish appreciation has come a long way since 1970, when Martin Paetz and I did our first edition of another book, *The Fishes of Alberta*.

I hope you enjoy this fine guide. You too can join the growing group of fish-lovers.

Joseph S. Nelson, Professor Emeritus, Department of Biological Sciences, University of Alberta, Edmonton. March 2003.

Lampreys & Sturgeons

Arctic Lamprey
page 50

Lake Sturgeon
page 52

Mooneyes

Goldeye
page 54

Mooneye
page 56

Minnows

Lake Chub
page 58

Western Silvery Minnow
page 60

Brassy Minnow
page 62

Pearl Dace
page 64

Emerald Shiner
page 66

River Shiner
page 68

Spottail Shiner
page 70

Northern Redbelly Dace
page 72

Finescale Dace
page 74

Fathead Minnow
page 76

Minnows

Flathead Chub
page 78

Northern Pikeminnow
page 80

Longnose Dace
page 82

Redside Shiner
page 84

Suckers

Quillback
page 86

Longnose Sucker
page 88

White Sucker
page 90

Largescale Sucker
page 92

Mountain Sucker
page 94

Silver Redhorse
page 96

Shorthead Redhorse
page 98

Catfishes & Pikes

Stonecat
page 100

Northern Pike
page 102

Trouts

Cisco
page 104

Shortjaw Cisco
page 106

Lake Whitefish
page 108

Pygmy Whitefish
page 110

Round Whitefish
page 112

Mountain Whitefish
page 114

Arctic Grayling
page 116

Cutthroat Trout
page 118

Rainbow Trout
page 120

Golden Trout
page 122

Brown Trout
page 124

Bull Trout
page 126

Brook Trout
page 128

Lake Trout
page 130

Trout-perches & Cods

Trout-perch
page 132

Burbot
page 134

Sticklebacks

Brook Stickleback
page 136

Ninespine Stickleback
page 138

Sculpins

Slimy Sculpin
page 140

Shorthead Sculpin
page 142

Spoonhead Sculpin
page 144

Deepwater Sculpin
page 146

Perches

Iowa Darter
page 148

Logperch
page 150

Yellow Perch
page 152

Sauger
page 154

Walleye
page 156

INTRODUCTION

A White Sucker rests camouflaged in its lakeside habitat.

B oating along one of Alberta's lakes or rivers, you may pause to wonder at nature's marvelous performances—birds singing, bugs buzzing, wind murmuring through the summer leaves. All of a sudden the cold slap of a fish's body re-entering the water snatches your eyesight from the trees, and the remaining ripples remind you that Mother Nature does not stop at the water's surface. Plenty of amazing things await your discovery in the depths of Alberta's wet places. We rarely think about the underwater realm, yet there is a meaningful connection between us and the fishes. Many of us were introduced to fishes with a small net and pail in our hands, catching "minnows" to watch them swim confused around their new world until we released them back to the wild. Just as people are easily mesmerized by a fish gliding through a backyard pond or aquarium, they are often even more intrigued by watching a fish in its natural environment.

This book is for anyone who appreciates fishes and wants to learn more about them. Anglers, boaters and nature enthusiasts will appreciate having this book in their collection. The introduction discusses fish biology, describes some of the challenges facing fishes in Alberta, introduces you to the practice of fishwatching and shows you how to identify fishes. The species accounts that follow describe in detail the lives of 54 Alberta fishes, and 11 other notable species are included in the appendix.

IDENTIFYING FISHES

One of the first things you will want to do after spotting a fish is to determine what species it is. Knowing the species of a fish opens the door to information about its food preferences, spawning habits and general biology. You may make some exciting discoveries. If you think you have found a species outside the range that is shown in this book, get some pictures of it or draw a quick sketch if you can. Biologists will be interested to hear of your find, and they will want to be able to verify your identification. Some species, such as the Arctic Lamprey

and the Deepwater Sculpin, have only been found in our province a few times.

There are 51 native species and 14 introduced species in Alberta, so determining the species of the fish you hold in your hand may not be an easy task. Lake Sturgeon and

Plenty of confusion surrounds the use of the words "fish" and "fishes." If more than one species of fish is being discussed, scientists use the term "fishes." If more than one individual of the same species is the topic, for example two Burbot, they say "two fish."

Arctic Lamprey are pretty distinctive, but identifying a minnow or a sculpin can be very difficult. Hybrids, between trout species especially, can also make determining the identity of a fish challenging. In most cases it is possible to accurately determine the species with careful consideration of the physical features discussed here. The key on page 36 will direct you to the correct family for most specimens, and it is followed by keys to determine exact species. Described below are many of the features that can be found on a fish, but note that not every fish will have all of the features mentioned here.

One of the first things to look at is a fish's mouth. Fishes with a **terminal mouth** have upper and lower jaws meeting at the tip of the snout. By contrast, when the upper and lower jaw meet behind the snout, the fish has a **subterminal mouth**. A mouth that is either terminal or subterminal can also be **oblique**, meaning that when looked at in a side view, the mouth angles down from the snout rather than extending horizontally. Fishes that feed on organisms found on the bottom of water bodies sometimes have a **fleshy, ventral mouth**. Both their upper and lower lips are placed on the underside of their bodies. Sometimes you will see structures that look like whiskers around the fish's mouth. These structures are called **barbels**; they act as "feelers" for fishes that live in darkened or silty water. During the spawning season, some members of the trout family, such as Brook Trout and Bull Trout, develop a **kype**, meaning that the upper and lower jaws are enlarged and hooked. This feature often develops in conjunction with increasingly brilliant coloration.

The placement and structure of a fish's fins are two of the most important traits in species identification. The **pectoral fins** are

Terminal mouth of Burbot

Oblique mouth of Mooneye

Subterminal mouth of Longnose Dace

Fleshy, ventral mouth of Longnose Sucker

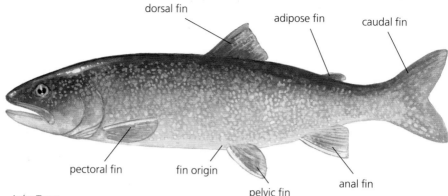

dorsal fin
adipose fin
caudal fin
pectoral fin
fin origin
pelvic fin
anal fin

Lake Trout

the fins closest to the mouth, and they can be on the side or underside of the fish. **Pelvic fins** are usually just beneath and behind the pectoral fins. Along the fish's back you will find the **dorsal fin**; some fishes such as perches have two dorsal fins. The **anal fin** is found on the ventral side of the fish, between the pelvic fins and the tail. The fin at the end of the tail is called the **caudal fin**. The end of the caudal fin can be forked or straight, or even asymmetrical, as with the Lake Sturgeon. The **adipose fin** can be found on members of the trout, bullhead catfish and trout-perch families. It is a small, rayless fin that is opposite the anal fin. **Rays** are the long structures that support most fin membranes. They can be hard and spiky (called **spines**) or soft and branching (called **soft rays**). Sometimes the number, length or type of rays on a fin is used to identify a fish species or gender.

The **lateral line** extends along the midsection of the fish on each side from the gills to the tail fin. When fishes in the trout family are young, dark, vertical **parr marks** may appear along the lateral line.

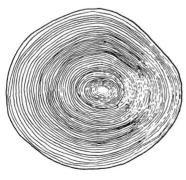

Cycloid scale

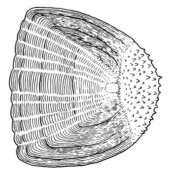

Ctenoid scale

A fish never stops growing; its growth just slows down once it becomes an adult. The number of scales a fish is born with does not change. The scales grow with the fish, developing "growth rings" like a tree.

Two types of scales can be found on the skin of Alberta fishes. Most of our fishes have **cycloid scales**, which are relatively smooth and circular. **Ctenoid scales** are found on more evolutionarily advanced fishes, such as perches. These scales have small spines and make the fish feel rough to the touch. Some of Alberta's fishes don't have scales. All of the sculpins, as well as the Stonecat and the Arctic Lamprey, lack scales. The Lake Sturgeon has what some would call modified scales: five rows of bony plates called **scutes** run along its body to create an armour that no other Alberta fish can match.

THE LIVES OF FISHES
LIFE STAGES
Fishes go through a number of stages before they become adults. When they hatch from their eggs, they still depend on their yolk sacs for nutrition. Once they have absorbed their yolk sacs the **larval stage** begins, and they are developed enough to capture food on their own.

There are two main strategies to producing young fishes: make a few big, tough kids with great survival abilities that require a lot of calories per egg, which might have been better used for growth; or play the lottery and produce millions of weak kids that have virtually no chance of survival but require very few calories per egg. Species such as trout follow the first strategy; the few eggs they produce are proportionally large in relation to adult body size (most of the extra bulk is yolk). Larvae of these species tend to have well-developed eyes and mouths and are able to swim efficiently at the beginning of the larval stage. They also have well-developed digestive systems that can extract up to 80 percent of the energy available in their food. Larvae of other species such as Walleye,

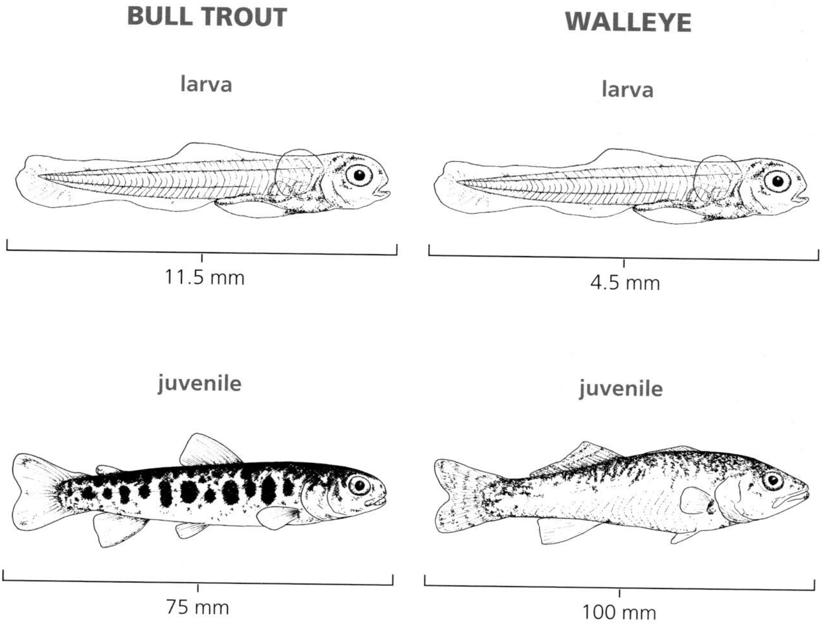

BULL TROUT

larva

11.5 mm

WALLEYE

larva

4.5 mm

juvenile

75 mm

juvenile

100 mm

A comparison of the average sizes of Bull Trout and Walleye as just-hatched larvae and as juveniles at the end of their first summer.

which follow the second strategy, have poorly developed eyes and mouths and can swim less efficiently. Despite these shortcomings, they must eat more food because their digestive systems are poorly developed; they can extract only 20 to 30 percent of the energy from their food. Because so many young are produced, some individuals are bound to be in the right places at the right times, successfully growing to maturity.

The incubation period for each species depends on many factors. Physiologically, fishes that release few high-quality eggs have a longer development period than species that release many low-quality eggs. To determine the incubation time of a species, fish biologists will raise eggs in the lab at a constant temperature. The amount of days it takes the eggs to hatch multiplied by the degrees Celsius of the water is the number of "degree days" for that species. For example, if the eggs in the lab were raised at 20° C and hatched in five days, then the number of degree days would be 100. With this result, fish biologists can determine how long it will take the eggs to hatch in any water temperature. If the same species of eggs in the wild was in water with a temperature of 10° C, it would take 10 days for them to hatch. This concept explains why there can be such great variation in the length of the incubation period within a species.

As with incubation, the length of the larval period varies among species and depends on temperature. The young are considered **juveniles** when they are basically identical to adults except that their reproductive organs

*Because members of the trout family are important to humans, their reproduction has been well studied and special terminology has developed. These fishes build gravel nests, called **redds**, in which they release their eggs. Young fishes are called **alevins** before they have fully absorbed their yolk sac and are called **fry** afterward. Alevins that emerge before their eggs sacs disappear are called **button-up fry**. Juveniles have a series of bars on their sides called **parr marks**.*

aren't mature. Once fishes are capable of breeding, they are considered **adults**. In the species accounts we focus on the biology of adult fishes because the biology of each stage can be very different. Fishes may eat different food and be found in different habitat at each stage, and it is beyond the scope of this book to include information for all life stages. Unless we specifically refer to larvae or juveniles, you can assume that we are discussing the biology of adults.

ACTIVITY PATTERNS

Feeding, followed closely by avoiding being another fish's meal, are high priorities, and fishes have a variety of anatomical and behavioural feeding adaptations. For example, suckers and sculpins, which feed along the bottom, have both jaws located on the underside of their bodies. In comparison, species that feed on insects at the surface of the water, such as the Goldeye and ciscoes, have their jaws located at the tip of their snouts, and their lower jaws may be longer than their upper jaws. Fishes also have different feeding habits—some carnivores ambush their prey, some are chasers and create suction to draw animals into their mouths. Fishes may also be nocturnal feeders, relying on the cover of darkness to hide from predators.

Fishes need rest, just like people do. They do not have eyelids, so they cannot close their eyes, but they enter a sleeplike period of deep relaxation in which very few stimuli will disrupt them (they can even be unaware of a diver's presence unless touched). Not surprisingly, most fishes find a place to hide while they are resting.

In winter, the lives of fishes change very little. The water under the ice is between 0° C and 4° C, and the fishes found in Alberta are so tolerant of cold that such temperatures in winter affect them very little. It is amazing to think that in Alberta, these cold-blooded animals can spawn and be most active at low temperatures, when other ectotherms, such as snakes and amphibians, are motionless lumps. The challenge for Alberta fishes at the end of the winter can be surviving low oxygen conditions. When a water body freezes over, the water is effectively sealed off from the atmosphere, and the amount of oxygen present in the water must maintain fishes and other aquatic animals until ice break-up in the spring. Because ice and snow cover block out most of the light, plants do not photosynthesize in winter, although sometimes there is a thin film of algae just under the ice. When oxygen levels are extremely low in late winter, some species, such as the Northern Pike, remain motionless just below the ice, taking advantage of the small amount of oxygen produced by the algae.

Winterkill, caused by lack of oxygen, is most common when a hot summer is followed by an early, snowy winter. The shallow water of many of Alberta's lakes promotes warming, which in turn provides a good environment for algae blooms. The decomposition of algae uses up oxygen. When the lack of photosynthesis in winter is combined with a lot of algae decomposition, all the oxygen can get used up more quickly, and fishes may suffocate—in effect, fishes can drown. Most of the time, winterkill is only partial, meaning that a few fishes will survive in special spots of higher oxygen. These surviving fishes can then quickly repopulate the lake. Sometimes complete winterkills occur. Then the lake depends on fishes swimming up creeks to repopulate the system.

SPAWNING

The spawning season is an intense time for fishes, often involving extraordinary risks. Some males become very eye-catching in their bright colours, not only to the females that they are trying to impress, but also to predators. The production of eggs and **milt** (the fish equivalent to semen) can require a lot of energy, and fishes that are spawning or searching for mates are often less wary. For the Arctic Lamprey and the Trout-perch, spawning is soon followed by death. Many other Alberta species spawn every year or every few years; the very long-lived Lake Sturgeon spawns once every two to seven years.

Fishes have a variety of spawning adaptations, and all methods are designed to keep the eggs healthy and surrounded by clean, oxygen-rich water. Some eggs are semi-buoyant so that they stay near the surface of the water and do not fall into the bottom of a silty river, and other eggs are adhesive so that they can attach to vegetation or rock surfaces above the suffocating silt of lake and river bottoms. Wave-swept beaches and fast, turbulent water below beaver dams and rapids are other favourite silt-free and oxygen-rich spawning sites. Some species build nests. Nests may be simply made when fishes brush away gravel and silt with their tails, as with trouts. Other species, such as sticklebacks, have intricate nesting behaviours.

In both species that build nests and species that don't, the eggs may be taken care of after spawning, usually by the male. He defends the eggs from predators and may also fan the eggs with his tail to make sure they receive enough oxygen or clean them off periodically with his mouth so they don't get coated with silt. Other species abandon the eggs after releasing them.

In some species, particularly the trouts, males defend territories during the breeding season and females mate with them within these territories. Larger males are able to bully smaller males out of the best territories, and small males may even be left without any breeding territory. Many small males find ways to continue their lineage by lying in wait and darting out as the female is releasing her eggs. They often have the opportunity to release milt before territorial males are aware of their presence. Deception in the mating season is not limited to males. A female may wander into a male's territory and grab a free meal of another female's fresh fish eggs while the

Fishes are the largest group of vertebrates, with about 25,000 living species. They have an incredible diversity of adaptations, from arctic fishes that don't freeze because of anti-freeze proteins in their blood, to lung-fishes that can remain dormant for up to four years in response to drought. Some fishes are also capable of producing electricity and light, others can leave the water and glide and fly.

male attempts to court her. Bill Griffiths Creek near Canmore is a great place for fishwatchers to see these rascally behaviours. In November, Brown Trout from the Bow River congregate here, within easy viewing distance of streamside trails.

ADAPTATIONS TO LIFE IN WATER
MOVEMENT

Water is 800 times denser than air, so it is not surprising that fishes have long, smooth, streamlined bodies that generally taper at the head and tail. Strong muscles along the length of the fish's body, especially in the tail, provide it with the power to propel itself in water. The caudal fin helps to give the tail strokes more power, and the single and paired fins along the fish's body help it with balance and steering. In addition, as anyone who has handled a fish would know, fishes' bodies are covered in mucus. This mucus reduces friction from movement in the water, and it also waterproofs the fish and helps to protect it from parasites and disease. Human skin is only semi-waterproof. We know it is not waterproof because after spending too long in water our skin gets "pruney." This peculiarity is caused by tiny amounts of water leaking in and swelling up our skin. Maybe if humans had a good mucous covering, we wouldn't get prune-skin when we swim.

Just as atmospheric pressure is greater at sea level than it is at the top of a mountain, water pressure increases with increasing depth. Many fish species have evolved a way to maintain neutral buoyancy in the water so that they don't have to expend as much energy to stay at a particular depth. These fishes have a **swim bladder**, which is a flexible gas-filled organ. Species that inhabit relatively shallow water have a duct that connects the swim bladder to the gut. They swallow air at the surface to fill the swim bladder. Species that frequent deeper water have evolved a different mechanism whereby gas from the blood enters and exits the swim bladder at a structure called the **gas gland**. When a fish descends in the water column, the increased pressure on the fish from the water surrounding it causes the gas in the bladder to compress. More gas diffuses into the swim bladder, and the weight of the extra gas causes the fish to become heavier. Conversely, when the fish moves upward in the water column, the decreased pressure on the fish causes the gas to expand, and excess gas diffuses out of the swim bladder back into the blood. The gas is then used by the body or removed from the blood at the gills. When fishes are swimming, they change depth slowly enough that the swim bladder has time to pressurize, but if deepwater fishes such as Walleye and Yellow Perch are pulled up too fast by anglers, the bladder can grow to a lethal size and compress the kidney or rupture itself.

BREATHING

Another challenge facing these aquatic animals is that water contains only 10 parts per million or less of oxygen compared to about 200,000 parts per million in air. As a result, fishes have evolved a highly efficient way of absorbing oxygen. They are able to remove about 80 percent of the oxygen in water, whereas humans remove only 10 to 20 percent of the oxygen in air. A fish takes water in through its mouth and closes its throat to push the water out through its **gills**. Inside each gill is a network of very thin-walled capillaries. Blood in these capillaries flows in the opposite direction as the water. As a result, the water always comes into contact with blood that has lower oxygen concentration than the water. Molecules always move from an area of high concentration to an area of low concentration, so the oxygen moves from the water to the blood. The carbon dioxide that is left over from respiration passes from the blood, where it is in high concentration, to the water. A bony gill cover, the **operculum**, protects the gills on the exterior of the fish, and long, thin, fleshy **gill rakers** block out particles drawn in with the water that may harm the delicate gill tissue. In some species the gill rakers are also used for filter-feeding. Fish-lovers must be very careful to avoid harming a fish's gills. Fish hooks or a misplaced finger can easily damage these delicate and critical organs, leaving

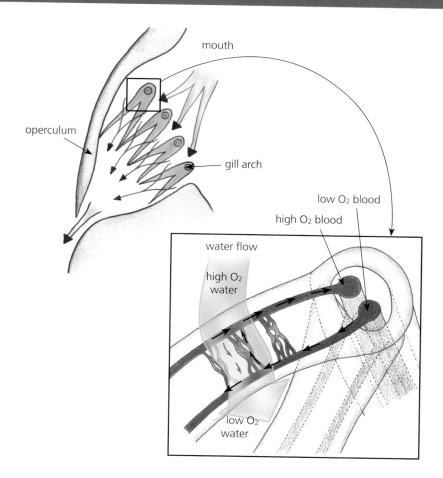

mouth

operculum

gill arch

low O$_2$ blood

high O$_2$ blood

water flow

high O$_2$ water

low O$_2$ water

the poor fish hemorrhaging or with impaired breathing.

THE SENSES

The animal kingdom is divided into **vertebrates** (animals with a spinal column) and **invertebrates** (animals without a spinal column). Like us, fishes are vertebrates. Overall, their sensory systems are similar to ours, but in some ways they are very different.

Because the eyes of fishes bulge out of their heads and because of the way the lens is positioned in the eyes, they are able to focus close up when they are looking forward and far away when they look out to the side. Fishes have the luxury of both binocular depth perception, which helps them to know exactly how far away a prey item or obstacle in front of them is, and the ability to watch for predators on both sides of their bodies at once. Most fishes can see in colour, although the Goldeye, which lives in very silty rivers, can see in only black and white, trading colour vision for excellent low light vision. The range of colours that fishes see depends on the depth of the water they are in. Red wavelengths are absorbed close to the surface of the water, while ultraviolet light can penetrate as far down as 100 metres in a clear, calm lake. Fishes that inhabit very deep water or very silty water must rely more on their other senses to find food and detect predators. The Stonecat lives in the murky water of the Milk River and must feel around with its barbels to make up for the poor visibility in its watery home.

Fishes sense taste in much the same way that we do, but the location of their taste buds is not limited to their mouths! The taste buds can also be located on "lips," barbels, fins and even skin. Fishes smell with the **nares** located at the tip of their snouts, and can often determine on which side of their bodies a substance is more concentrated. The sense of smell is important for helping fishes find prey, and also for detecting **pheromones** (hormones released into the environment that produce a response in individuals of the same species), which are particularly important in the spawning season. Sense of smell is also thought to direct fishes during spawning migrations.

Water is an excellent conductor of sound. You may notice when you put your head underwater that sounds seem different— sound vibrations travel farther and faster in water. As vibrations move through the water, they move the water back and forth, and the body of a fish naturally moves with the water. Three ear stones, called **otoliths**, in the fish's inner ear sense these movements in a similar way that our ear ossicles sense the sound that is channelled to our ear drums. High-frequency sounds, however, are not easily picked up by movements of the body, because water is displaced less by high frequencies. Fishes that have a swim bladder can detect high frequencies better than fishes without a swim bladder, because the air in

*Many fishes have dark-coloured backs that grade to light-coloured undersides. This coloration is called **countershading**. When viewed from above, the dark colour helps the fish to blend into the darkness of the water below it. Similarly, the pale underside blends in well with the lighter water above the fish when it is seen from below.*

the swim bladder pulsates in response to sound. These pulsations vibrate the body tissues of the fish, and the vibrations are picked up by the inner ear. The closer the swim bladder is positioned to the inner ear, the better the fish can hear high-frequency sounds. Some fishes, such as minnows and catfishes, have evolved a chain of small bones called **Weberian ossicles**, which efficiently transmit vibrations from the swim bladder to the inner ear.

Fishes sense temperature changes and physical touch through their skin. In addition, cells called **neuromasts** enable them to sense water movements. Neuromasts can be found anywhere on the surface of a fish, but many of them are found along the lateral line. The ability to sense water movements can help a fish detect the movements of predators or prey, and it can also help them to avoid obstacles and maintain schooling behaviour in poorly lit situations.

THE UNDERWATER WORLD

Although water seems to be a uniform medium, the world that fishes inhabit is anything but simple. Oxygen content and water temperature can vary greatly among different habitats. Some water bodies are very clear and allow a lot of light penetration, whereas others are very silty. The strength of water currents also varies. In addition, the bottom of a water body may be rocky, sandy or silty, and shallow areas may or may not be well vegetated. Boulders, fallen trees and vegetation along the shore and on the bottom offer fishes many places from which to ambush prey or hide from predators.

One of the variables that affects fishes the most in summer is temperature. Fishes are ectothermic (cold-blooded) animals, which means that their body temperature varies with the temperature fluctuations of their environment. Whereas the body temperature of a human is approximately 37° C no matter what the outside temperature is, the body temperature of a fish is exactly the same as its environment whether ambient temperature is 18° C or 4° C.

The activity level of a fish generally increases with water temperature, although water that is too warm can cause a fish to slow down. A fish is healthiest and can usually swim most efficiently within its preferred temperature range. In Alberta, fishes are classified into coldwater species and coolwater species. **Coldwater fishes**, such as many trout species, prefer summer water temperatures between 10° C and 18° C. Many other Alberta species are **coolwater fishes**, which prefer summer water temperatures between 18° C and 26° C.

LAKES

In summer, the water in a lake settles into layers, with the warmest, most oxygen-rich water at the surface and the coldest, most oxygen-poor water at the bottom. In many lakes, coolwater species inhabit the surface of a lake, and coldwater species are found along the bottom.

Relatively shallow, bowl-shaped lakes such as those in our grassland and aspen parkland regions are usually the most productive. Quite often these shallow lakes started as deep lakes and have been filled in with sediments over time. The sediments are high in nutrients, which encourage plant growth. Increased plant growth, in turn, provides a more complex habitat and often results in the presence of a greater number of animals. The long, gently sloping shoreline also provides more area along which rooted plants can grow. Deep, V-shaped lakes, such as those found in the mountains and

foothills, often have much steeper shorelines so that the area of depth at which rooted plants have sufficient light to grow is more limited. These lakes are low in nutrients.

Within any lake there are **littoral** (shoreline), **pelagic** (open-water) and **benthic** (deepwater and bottom) areas. All rooted vegetation is found along the shoreline. Species that spawn in lakes usually move to shorelines to breed, because the water is oxygen-rich and warm and because vegetation provides cover for the eggs and juvenile fishes. Large predators are also less likely to frequent the shallows because of their size. Many small fishes, such as members of the minnow family, are often found in the littoral area as well. Away from the shoreline, the pelagic area of a lake is home to fishes that feed on plankton and to predators of plankton feeders. **Plankton** is the term given to microscopic organisms that live in water. The benthic area is home to species that feed on **detritus** (dead plant and animal matter) and, of course, the predators of detritus feeders.

As summer moves into autumn, temperature changes encourage mixing of the water in a lake. The layers dissolve and the temperature and oxygen content become uniform. Water is heaviest at 4° C, so in the winter, when ice covers the lake, the 4° C water sinks to the bottom of the lake and the colder water sits on top. In spring, the water mixes again producing uniform temperature and oxygen content before summer stratification begins again.

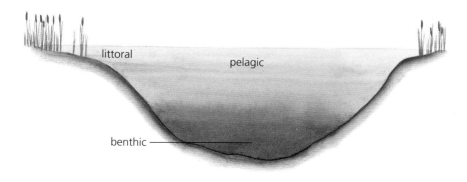

The three major habitats for fishes within a water body.

Open water in winter

RIVERS

In rivers, oxygen content and temperature don't vary much in relation to depth, but they do vary as the water gets farther from its source. Headwater rivers are usually fast-flowing, coldwater streams, and because of the rapids and rocky shallows splashing and mixing the water, they are generally oxygen-rich. Their bottoms are usually rocky and often low in nutrients. These headwater rivers unite to form larger rivers, which are joined by tributaries and become still larger, and on and on until the largest river finally

meets the ocean. The gradient of rivers often decreases as they move out of higher areas onto flatter land, and as a result, water movement becomes slower. As rivers move away from their source and get larger, the water also generally gets warmer, and nutrient availability increases so plant growth is generally more abundant. Larger rivers generally have a higher silt load and, as a result, can get very murky.

Rivers are less affected by the seasons than lakes are. Many of the larger rivers freeze over in winter, but the water under the ice keeps flowing. Parts of mountain streams may even stay open throughout the year, providing sources of much-needed oxygen and great viewing sites for hardy fishwatchers.

ALBERTA HABITAT

Streams and lakes in this province cover 16,796 square kilometres, which may sound like a lot but amounts to a mere trickle compared to the rest of the country. Alberta has the least amount of fresh water of all the territories and provinces except for the Maritime provinces; only 2.5 percent of Alberta's surface is covered by water. Despite this lack of surface water, Alberta's rivers drain into two out of the three oceans that surround Canada. Most of the province's water flows north to the Mackenzie River, spilling out into the Arctic Ocean. Water from the North Saskatchewan River and South Saskatchewan River drains into Hudson Bay, eventually mixing with Atlantic Ocean waters. The southern Atlantic Ocean is also touched by Alberta's water via the Milk River, which just peeks into the southeastern corner of Alberta

Alberta's cold climate is the single-most important feature of our fish habitat. Seven months of ice cover and relatively cool summers means fishes here grow very slowly compared to fishes elsewhere in North America. Walleye become adults at two years of age in the southern part of their range, but they don't reach adult size until they are 8 to 10 years old here! Also, some Lake Trout in high mountain lakes are only about 30 cm long after 20 years.

DRAINAGE BASINS OF ALBERTA

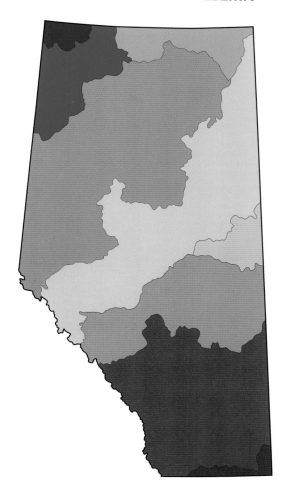

Arctic Ocean Drainage
- Liard River Basin
- Hay River Basin
- Peace River Basin
- Slave River Basin
- Athabasca River Basin

Hudson Bay Drainage
- Churchill River Basin
- North Saskatchewan River Basin
- South Saskatchewan River Basin

Gulf of Mexico Drainage
- Milk River Basin

The common fishes of boreal rivers are Longnose Suckers, Flathead Chub and Walleye.

majority of our large river basins, including the Peace, Athabasca, Slave, Hay and Liard rivers. Spruce and aspen forests and low wetlands, such as muskegs and bogs, characterize this region. Unlike much of the rest of Canada, only a small portion of Alberta's northern lands are underlain by the rocky Precambrian Shield. Most of northern Alberta is ancient sea-bottom from the time of the dinosaurs and before. This geological oddity means that although Alberta has much oil and gas, clear lakes and rocky streams are rare. Shallow, algae-covered lakes and muddy, sluggish creeks are the common fish habitat in the boreal forest. Huge variation in climate is normal, with droughts mixed with floods and dry winters mixed with huge snowfalls. Boreal fishes are well adapted to these conditions through specialized behaviours and tolerances to conditions such as heavy silt, low oxygen and large temperature changes. Many of these fishes can migrate into fringe areas, such as ponds and small creeks, when conditions are good (e.g., high water, good temperatures)

and eventually joins up with the great Mississippi River to run into the Gulf of Mexico.

Alberta's landmass can be divided into four large ecoregions, each with specific climates, geology and vegetation that influence the aquatic world. The largest area by far is occupied by **Boreal Forest**. It contains the

Look for Spottail Shiners, Lake Whitefish and White Suckers in boreal lakes.

and leave for larger rivers and lakes when times are bad. People have also expanded into Alberta's boreal forest, mainly chasing lumber and petrochemicals, but finding great fishing for Walleye and other perches, Northern Pike and Arctic Grayling. Unfortunately, heavy human access has often meant too many fish dinners, and consequently many boreal populations have declined. Other populations remain healthy, and travellers to a few far reaches of the north can still see almost pristine fish communities.

Cottages dot the lakeshores in the **Aspen Parkland**. Fish habitat in this region is characterized by a few large, shallow lakes, such as Lac Ste. Anne, Wabamun and Pigeon. Smaller rivers drain into the North Saskatchewan River, in which about half of Alberta's fishes are found. To the east, the Beaver River comprises Alberta's small contribution to the Churchill River Basin. Although biologically similar to the fish communities of the boreal forest, variation in floods and droughts, decades of fishing by settlers,

Yellow Perch, Emerald Shiners and Northern Pike live in parkland lakes.

commercial fishers and cottagers, and stocking of species such as Rainbow Trout have reshaped these aspen parkland fish communities. Laws reducing pollution and protecting habitat have allowed recovery of many of these fish populations. Urban centres such as Edmonton and Red Deer can now boast diverse and recovering fisheries.

Parkland ponds are good places to look for Fathead Minnows and Brook Sticklebacks.

Common species in grassland rivers include Goldeye and Longnose Suckers.

The **Grasslands** are better known for being dry than wet, and the water bodies here are few. Slow-moving rivers and warm potholes characterize this region. Any water is potentially fish habitat, and irrigation canals and ditches are able to shelter many small fishes of the prairies. Oddly enough, the huge irrigation reservoirs that have been constructed can be great habitat for certain fishes. These lakes, such as Newell, McGregor and Tilley, now support some of Alberta's largest commercial fisheries for Lake Whitefish. In the arid plains, pothole lakes with very little inflow and high evaporation can have high salinity. Fishes such as the Fathead Minnow have adapted to these conditions and are sometimes the only fish species to survive in salty potholes. The Red Deer, Bow and Oldman rivers, which run through the grasslands, are tributaries of the South Saskatchewan River. In the southeastern tip of Alberta is the Milk River, which got its name because of its silty appearance. There are very few rocky shores in the grasslands; shorelines are usually sand, clay or a mixture of both.

Fishes that are unique to grassland rivers are Western Silvery Minnows and Stonecats.

Look for Mountain Whitefish and Brook Trout in mountain rivers.

The **Mountains** and **Foothills** of the west contain many fast-flowing streams that are fed with boundless energy by the immense glaciers that cloak the Rockies. The cold, clear lakes that dot the valleys house slow-growing fish, such as Lake Trout and Bull Trout. The headwaters of most of Alberta's rivers occur in the Rockies. Many of Alberta's native trout species are here and are well adapted to seasonal floods with glacial silt, brief productive summers and cold, long winters. The clear, shallow water makes for some of the best trout-watching in the province, as many an avid fly fisher will attest.

Mountain rivers provide the best opportunities for viewing Pygmy Whitefish and Bull Trout.

TOP ALBERTA FISHWATCHING SITES

BOREAL FOREST

1. Slave River, in back-flooded marshes at Fitzgerald
2. Peace River, at the bridge by Dunvegan
3. Gregoire Lake, at the beach in the provincial park and at the dam on the outlet river by Anzac
4. House River, at the bridge on Highway 63
5. Lesser Slave Lake, at the beach at Shaw's Point
6. Lac La Biche, along the causeway to Churchill Park
7. Touchwood Lake, at the stream right in the campground
8. Sand River, under the bridge on Highway 55
9. Cold Lake, at the marina in front of the townsite

ASPEN PARKLAND

10. Sturgeon River, where it leaves Lac Ste. Anne and along the trails behind the Arden Theatre in St. Albert
11. Wabamun Lake, at the big dock in the town
12. North Saskatchewan River, at Devon, near the Muttart Conservatory in Edmonton and at the storm-water outlet about 200 metres upstream of the Groat Road bridge on the north side of the river
13. Whitemud Creek, in Edmonton, both at the creek mouth near Fort Edmonton and along the hiking trails upstream
14. Astotin Lake, at the campground in Elk Island National Park
15. Vermilion River, along the trails by the reservoir in the town of Vermilion
16. Tide Creek, on the northwest shore of Pigeon Lake
17. Coal Lake, by the culvert under Highway 616
18. Battle River, at the Highway 850 crossing

GRASSLANDS

19. Red Deer River, at the Highway 36 bridge and at the Highway 884 bridge
20. Berry Creek, where it flows into the Red Deer River near Dinosaur Provincial Park
21. Travers Reservoir, in the Little Bow Provincial Park at the beach by the boat launch
22. Little Bow River, by the Tipi Ring Site north of Carmangay on Highway 23
23. Oldman River, along the trails in Lethbridge
24. Milk River, in Writing-on-Stone Provincial Park

MOUNTAINS AND FOOTHILLS

25. Freeman River, west of Highway 33 in the Swan Hills
26. Little Smoky River, at the bridge by Grizzly Junction
27. Rock Lake, at the outlet near the south campground
28. Sundance Creek, alongside Highway 16, west of Edson
29. Pyramid Lake, along the boardwalk to the island
30. Beauvert Lake, at the dock at the Jasper Park Lodge and along the lakeshore trails
31. Maligne River, under the bridge, where it leaves Maligne Lake
32. Sunwapta River, near mouths of tiny, unnamed tributaries along the Icefields Parkway, generally near Beauty Creek
33. Shunda Creek, both in the creek and along the beaver ponds at the campground next to Highway 11
34. Onion Creek, which is a tributary of the upper South Ram River
35. Cave and Basin Marsh, at the hotsprings in Banff National Park (the weirdest site in Alberta!)
36. Bill Griffiths Creek, in the Bow Valley near Canmore, along Highway 1A
37. Smith-Dorrien Creek, where it flows into Lower Kananaskis Lake
38. Upper Crowsnest River, along Highway 3 above the dam

TOP SNORKELLING SITES

A. Touchwood Lake (Northern Pike, Walleye and White Suckers)
B. Cold Lake (Lake Trout in autumn)
C. Spring Lake, west of Edmonton (Yellow Perch)
D. Twin Lakes, west of Pigeon Lake (Yellow Perch, Northern Pike and Rainbow Trout)
E. McLeod River, upstream of Edson (Mountain Whitefish, Burbot, Walleye and Longnose Suckers)

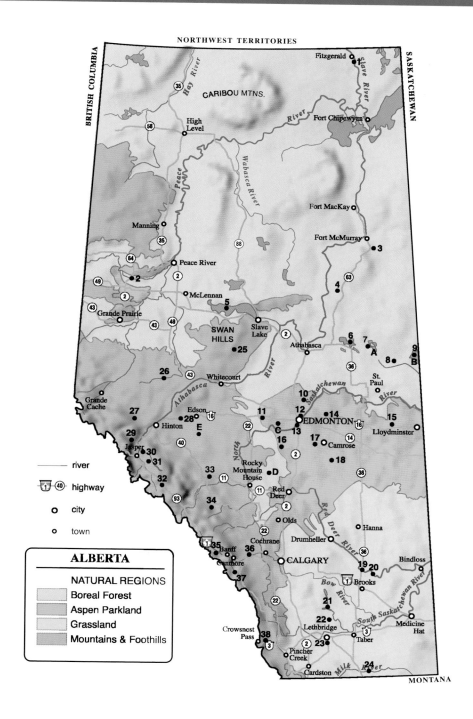

THE HISTORY OF FISHES IN ALBERTA

With 65 species, Alberta has approximately one-third of the number of species found in Ontario and only one-fifth of the number of species found in some states. Cold, long winters and short summers are partly responsible for our low number of fish species. Other reasons include the low amount of surface water—Alberta contains only 2.2 percent of Canada's fresh water—and the glacial history of the province.

The most recent ice age occurred from 24,000 years ago until about 13,000 years ago. During this time, all of Alberta, except the Cypress Hills and an area in the extreme southwestern portion of the province, was covered by ice. Prior to this ice age, fishes occupied Alberta; in fact, fishes have been present here, on and off, for many millions of years. The fishes that occur in Alberta today, however, have only been present since about 13,000 years ago. They are generally species that have great dispersal capabilities, and many of the species in Alberta are also present throughout Canada. They travelled to our province from three drainage basins that were free of ice during the ice age. Over two-thirds of the fishes that are native to our province travelled from the Missouri–Mississippi drainage basin of the southeastern United States, and the rest of our native species, with one exception, originated from the Columbia drainage basin of the northwestern United States. There was a small unglaciated area in the Yukon during the ice age, and it is from this area that the Arctic Lamprey entered our province. Some fishes likely entered by more than one route, making for interesting subpopulations, weird disjunct distributions and enough questions to keep generations of icthyologists happily puzzled and studying this fascinating topic.

In the last few centuries, humans have also contributed to the dispersal of fishes. Humans introduced 13 current Alberta species either on purpose or by accident. Three of these species are tropical fishes that inhabit the warm water of the Cave and Basin Hotsprings in Banff, and many of the others are trout species that were introduced as sport fishes.

CONSERVATION ISSUES

People like to eat fish. In Alberta, recreational anglers fish for many species, commercial fishers set gill-nets and First Nations people exercise ancient traditional values and treaty rights in catching fishes for subsistence use. Fish populations are usually not harmed when a few fishes are harvested. After all, these animals have supported Alberta food webs for millennia (bears, otters, minks, eagles and humans are just a few species that eat fishes). However, our cold climate results in slow growth and late maturity of fishes. Because Alberta fishes have very low productivity, only a relatively limited number of fishes can be safely and sustainably taken. If the harvest is too big, anglers will first notice that the size of the fishes in their catch is declining. This stage of overharvesting is called **growth overfishing** and is a sign that fishes aren't surviving as long as they once did and trouble is on the horizon. When this pattern is noticed early and the proper measures are taken (usually simply reducing the harvest), the fish population will quickly recover. If this pattern isn't noticed early or if effective measures aren't taken, the situation will get worse and the fishery may collapse. **Recruitment overfishing** occurs when adult fish numbers have declined to the point where spawning is often failing and few young fishes are being born. Anglers will still be able to catch fishes (especially if they know the best spots), but at this stage, the overall quality of the fishery is merely a shadow of its former self.

Unfortunately in Alberta, collapses have occurred with several species, at quite a few lakes and rivers. Certain populations of Lake Trout, Bull Trout, Cutthroat Trout, Walleye, Lake Sturgeon, Northern Pike and Yellow Perch have experienced heavy fishing pressure relative to their low biological productivity. Some of these populations have even been completely eliminated from the lake or river (called **extirpation**). Lake Trout in Touchwood Lake and Lesser Slave Lake were overfished so heavily that they no longer

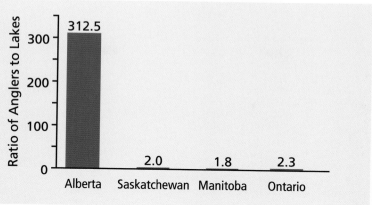

The number of Alberta anglers for each lake in the province is over 300.

exist in these lakes. Other examples of extirpations include Walleye in North Buck Lake and Wabamun Lake and native Alberta Cutthroat Trout in many foothill streams.

Over 350,000 anglers on 800 lakes can make a large dent in fish populations if we are not careful. Furthermore, the number of anglers reflects only licenced anglers; people over 65 do not require licenses. Since the 1980s, Alberta's lakes have seen an enormous increase in fishing. Wolf Lake, north of Bonnyville, has seen a 600 percent increase in anglers in the past 20 years, which has resulted in a sharp decrease of Walleye in the lake.

FISHERIES MANAGEMENT

It is the function of fisheries biologists to recognize the signs of overfishing and to prevent fish populations from declining. However, Alberta is a very large province with few biologists, and overharvests have usually gone unnoticed or unrecognized. Even when the first signs of overfishing were detected (for example, a decline in the size of fishes), these signs were often considered a desirable response to what were considered in those days to be good management practices. In most of North America, a concept called **Maximum Sustainable Yield** guided fisheries managers throughout much of the 1950s to 1980s. Based on fairly simple mathematics, this concept suggested that the largest harvest of fish of a certain species could be

taken when a fish population was reduced to about half of its unexploited level. Although the mathematics were correct, this concept failed to include real-world complexities, such as infrequent monitoring, variable spawning success and the strong reluctance of anglers to reduce their catches when times were bad. Now seen as an unfortunate step in the history of fisheries management, Maximum Sustainable Yield did teach biologists many important lessons about the importance of nature's variability and social factors in fisheries management.

From these hard-earned lessons rose the concept of **Precautionary Management**. In simple terms, this concept redesigned the mathematics of fisheries management to

Alberta's relatively low number of rivers and lakes and our cold climate means that we have few fishes that grow very slowly, with very high human fishing pressure. Fisheries scientists have said that if freshwater fisheries collapse anywhere in North America, it will happen first in Alberta, and it will hit hardest and take the longest time to recover here. This potentially disastrous combination of conditions has led fish biologists from all across Canada and the United States to watch and learn from the methods Albertans use to preserve our fish heritage.

include all those nasty variables, such as uncertainty about spawning success, climate change and unpredictable fishing pressure. Sustainable harvest levels were considerably reduced from the levels in the era of Maximum Sustainable Yield, and fisheries management plans were designed to be changed quickly and effectively, as nature and harvesting pressure dictated. During the 1990s, the conceptual and practical changes inherent in replacing Maximum Sustainable Yield with Precautionary Management created challenges for fisheries biologists and anglers alike. Computer models became commonplace, with complex mathematics and new concepts. Anglers saw very different fishing rules, usually including severe restrictions of catches.

Happily, the result of these difficult changes is a surge in many of Alberta's fish populations to levels unseen since our grandparents' time. Walleye and Northern Pike in many lakes have recovered to provide fishing quality usually only seen at remote fly-in fishing lodges. Although anglers can't keep nearly as many fishes as they once did, they can catch far more—and much larger—fishes than they ever remember. It will be a new challenge for Alberta fish-lovers to recognize the fragile nature of these recoveries and strive to avoid the mistakes of the past.

A young fish-lover holding a Northern Pike.

HABITAT CONSERVATION

"Without habitat, there would be no fish," is a common cliché heard around biologists' coffee rooms. In Alberta, much of the effort of fisheries biologists has traditionally gone toward protecting our waters from industrial pollution, shoreline destruction and other detrimental effects caused by people who don't know or care about the special needs of fishes. Especially during the 1950s and 1960s, the industrial expansion of Alberta created real problems, such as effluent in our rivers, silt pouring from stream crossings that were built too quickly and the mess of an exploding oil and gas industry. Lots of dedicated work has resolved many of these problems. Our large rivers have been cleaned up wonderfully, and localized oil spills or silt plumes are now quickly detected and stopped. Much work continues. Cottagers are being taught the importance of shoreline plants in creating fish spawning and nursery habitat and are turning down opportunities to build unnatural and expensive artificial beaches or concrete shorelines. Ranchers are learning about the economic benefits of keeping riparian areas (stream banks and lakeshores) untrammeled and healthy, not just for fishes, but for cattle and wildlife as well. Forestry and petrochemical companies know about the problems caused by culverts becoming impassable waterfalls and preventing fish migrations, and about roads eroding into fish spawning beds. Although these problems still occur, our society is rapidly learning how to have a lighter footprint and include a healthy environment as part of an economic bottom line.

WHAT CAN FISH-LOVERS DO TO HELP FISHES?

Become informed and take an interest in your local waters and fishes. What species live in that storm-water pond? Did fishes ever swim up this ditch past my driveway? Was that beaver pond ever fish habitat? By simply looking at the world around you and asking fishy questions, you'll become aware of possible threats to our finny friends. If fishes are in that stormwater pond, does the runoff from my street have nasty chemicals that might harm them? If so, why not start a "Yellow Fish Road" campaign. Paint yellow fish silhouettes on the sewer covers to let people know that this sewer drains into a fish's home. They may think twice before draining the car's used oil or putting pesticides on their lawn if they know where the runoff is going. Perhaps fishes once swam up a local ditch (before it was a ditch) to get to a great spawning marsh. Ask old-timers in your community of they ever saw such a thing. Maybe it can become fish habitat once again if that hanging culvert is replaced, or if a connection is remade to the big river. Lobby your local politicians or local biologist to make these improvements to your neighbourhood environment. If you see a problem, act. Bulldozers on shorelines, weird colours in river waters and sand being dumped on somebody's "beach" can all be signs of fish habitat destruction. Canadian provincial and federal governments have powerful laws, with enforcement staff and biologists specifically assigned to protect fish habitat. You can help by being a habitat watcher, as well as a fish-lover. Learn and teach. Help others become aware of the presence of fishes, their special needs and their value as touchstones of nature.

FISHWATCHING

Fishwatching is not yet a popular sport. Sad, but true. Fishes, as "lower vertebrates" in most people's eyes, just don't have the mass appeal of big-eyed deer fawns and majestic bull elk. But, consider birdwatchers. They comprise one of the biggest and most rapidly growing segments of the natural-history crowd. They spend millions on trips to bizarre locations, expensive binoculars, localized books and goofy hats. Fishwatchers can do all this too! Becoming a fishwatcher just involves learning a set of new "watching" techniques, investing in some simple equipment and getting bit by the fish bug. If nothing else, it gives you a good excuse to get off the couch, see some new landscapes and even meet other nature-lovers.

FISHWATCHING TECHNIQUES

The pioneer guru of Alberta's fishwatchers, Wayne Roberts, once said, "fly rods are to fishwatching what binoculars are to birdwatching." Certainly, angling is the most common and, likely, the most effective way to see a fish. All fishes must eat; therefore, with enough skill, all fishes should be catchable. Anyone can catch Northern Pike, Walleye and trouts, but consider the challenge of catching a Longnose Dace or being able to consistently hook a tough-mouthed stickleback. For most of our smaller species, use tiny flies (18s and smaller are the norm), trying to match the common plankton you see on the lake or river bottom. Super-light tippets and two-weight fly rods are standard equipment if your quarry is shiners, sculpins, daces and chubs. The joy in catching one of these tiny jewels is not in their sporting qualities (no one brags

Walleye spawning in a small stream.

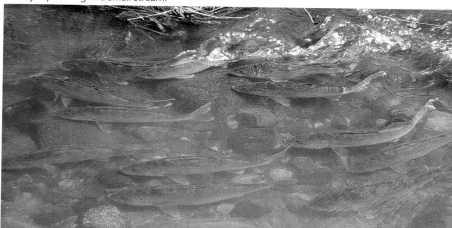

about the great fight from a Lake Chub), but in the simple reward of having persistence and skill pay off. More robust angling gear is useful on Alberta's larger rivers, when a small baited hook lying on the bottom will perhaps reward you with one of several colourful suckers, sparkling Flathead Chub or wriggly Burbot (besides the usual sport fishes). When angling, be prepared to handle fishes. Have a plastic dishpan of water ready to harmlessly hold the fish, keep longnose pliers or forceps handy for quick unhooking and be nice to the fish. Hold it gently, with wet hands, but not for long. How long can you keep a fish out of water? A good rule of thumb is to hold your breath. When you have to breathe, the fish probably wants to breathe also. Let it go, into the dishpan if you want a photo or a better look, and quickly back into the lake when you're finished.

Netting is also a good fishwatching technique. Aquarium dip nets are fine, but to maximize capture efficiency you'll need to duct-tape a longer willow stick to the handle. On warm summer days, is there anything as fun as splashing and chasing minnows in the shallows? If your reputation is too stolid and mature for such frivolous sport, borrow a neighbour's kid and blame the nonsense on them. ("Oh…well…you see, I was just teaching this child about aquatic ecosystem function, I wasn't having a water fight.")

More high-tech than dip nets are seine nets. You can purchase a short "minnow net" from most angling stores. Local laws usually allow anglers to catch minnows for bait, so fishwatchers can take advantage of this loophole and use a seine net to capture the more elusive fishes. Two people are needed to seine fishes, each person holding one end of the net.

"Does it hurt a fish when it is hooked?" is a question usually posed to fish biologists. Generally, the answer is yes, hence the thrashing about on the hook. But most of the stress from a catch and release results from being held out of the water. Some fishes may die from being hooked, but if care is taken in removing the hook and handling the fish, the likelihood of death is lessened.

Slowly walk along the shallows with the net trailing between you in a shallow "U" shape. After a short stroll (5 to 20 metres is typical), gently pull the net up onto a smooth shoreline and see the treasures scooped up in the base of the net. As with angling, be prepared to handle fishes before you start seining. A plastic tub or a bucket of water should be ready. Admire your catches; then release them back into their home. You may be tempted to keep a few beautiful specimens for your home aquarium. Please don't. Horror stories of unwanted fish introductions are too common in the fish world. People take fishes home, often a long way from the capture site. After some time, they decide to release the fishes into a local lake or river, which often is not the fish's natural habitat. The result is an introduced species and a potential ecological disaster. Most places have laws against moving live fishes for precisely this reason. Even if your jurisdiction doesn't have such a law, it is just being a good natural-world citizen to leave animals in their natural habitat.

Fishwatching doesn't have to involve angling or using nets to catch fishes. It can be as simple as peering over a bridge railing or as complex as stalking up to a pool in camouflage gear with a pair 9x32 polarized binoculars. Water reflects light, so viewing can be tricky, but polarized sunglasses are a great help. Pick your location. Looking down helps (stand on bridges, high riverbanks or on a dock), as does having the sun at your back. Fishwatching is a great hobby—it is best practised on calm, sunny days. Cloudy days are not great, and neither are windy or rainy days.

The spawning season is a good time for "hands-off" fishwatching. When it gets dark, rocky shallows come alive with Walleye and suckers spawning in the shallows. Fountainlike spray sometimes results from the large amount of thrashing about during spawning. Gently lift up any garbage that may be floating on a lakeshore, perhaps a Fathead Minnow has used it for a nesting site. If so, don't stay too long, because the male Fathead is sure to be very worried about his brood.

Binoculars are helpful for seeing the details on a fish, but they have to be modified for fishwatching by adding a polarized filter. Reverse porro-prism binoculars are the best choice for fishwatching—the two eyepiece lenses are farther apart than the two objective lenses. Fit a single polarizing filter for a large camera lens over the objective lenses using a rubber sunshade to hold the filter and a couple of elastic bands to hold the filter/sunshade over the binocular lens. By looking at the water through the binoculars and turning the filter, you can find the "sweet spot" and eliminate most of the glare. Suddenly, the fish will be close, clear and beautiful, and you'll be the one who is forever hooked. Fancy modifications include a close-up lens attached to the polarizing filter for focusing on nearby minnows.

Fish photography should be a natural addition to fishwatching, but it is actually one of the most difficult types of nature photography. The natural cryptic coloration of most fishes, as well as watery shimmer and glare make clear photos almost impossible to achieve. Bringing a fish out of the water helps somewhat, but the fins flop down, the fish looks like it is gasping, and shiny scales and wet skin give photographers a nightmare of exposure trouble. When you do try fish photos (and you should try), expect to take lots of shots, using a variety of exposures

"Why do fish jump?" is a question often posed to biologists. The answer may be different for some species than it is for others. Insectivorous fishes may overestimate their velocity when they reach for a floating bug, propelling themselves farther out of the water than necessary. Smaller fishes may also jump to avoid the jaws of a hungry predator. Sometimes it appears that fishes just jump for joy. Why else would a huge Lake Sturgeon leap from its deepwater world or would spawning suckers twirl from the water?

and angles. If you're lucky, one or two pictures will turn out, and they'll be gems.

Underwater fish viewing and photography by snorkelling or scuba diving are popular in the tropical oceans but are less suited to Alberta's cold, somewhat murky water. A few spots have good visibility for divers, but these tend to be the coldest (and often the most fishless) lakes around. Ask around at local dive shops for hot tips and refer to the snorkelling sites listed on the Top Alberta Fishwatching Sites map (page 26). Snorkelling along shallow weedbeds on summer days usually produces a few close-up views of

A set of binoculars modified for fishwatching (left); the separate parts (right).

An extreme fishwatcher on the prowl.

Yellow Perch or a motionless Northern Pike, but the big vistas of underwater reefs, teeming with fishes, that you see on T.V. shows from Hawaii just don't happen in Alberta.

Remote underwater video cameras are a new technology that holds promise for viewing fish. A small waterproof camera is lowered below your boat (or through an ice-fishing hole), with a video cable running up to a small television monitor. These cameras have special low-light abilities and can produce totally cool scenes of grey, ghostly fishes cruising through a murky world. Most high-end sport fishing stores carry a few models. These cameras may be the next big thing in fishwatching, and the cost is dropping as their popularity increases.

FISHWATCHING ETHICS

As true nature-lovers, fishwatchers should always adopt a lighter footprint approach to the sport. Be careful when handling fishes, get informed and follow all local fishing regulations. Don't disturb spawning fishes or fishes that are already stressed by unusually hot weather or low water. Even light-walkers can love special areas to death, so take care to stay on streamside trails and avoid stirring up unnecessary silt and mud. Be friendly to other fish-lovers by smiling and by happily avoiding a fly fisher's pool or a stream-bank angler's beach. The sport of fishing has traditional ethics designed to

avoid conflicts, such as leaving a pool after hooking a fish, fishing from the head to the tail of a run and exiting and reeling in lines if someone else hooks up. Fishwatchers should be no different and should display tolerance, formal politeness and, generally, be paradigms of nature-lover virtues (and splash around in the shallows a lot).

ABOUT THE SPECIES ACCOUNTS

This book gives detailed accounts of 54 fishes that are well established in Alberta. An extra 11 unusual fishes, species introduced to very restricted spots or just peeking into Alberta from their home ranges in other provinces are in the appendix. The order of fishes and their scientific names follow *The Fishes of Alberta* by J.S. Nelson and M.J. Paetz (1992), except a few changes made since 1992 that follow a draft document of the American Fisheries Society *Common and Scientific Names of Fishes* by J.S. Nelson et al.

Each account includes the following information.

VIEWING TIPS: A species is often more likely to be seen in certain places, and there are often specific signs of its presence. This section lets you know where to look and what to look for to get acquainted with a particular species.

FEEDING: In this section we mention the kinds of things that adult fishes eat and the way they forage. The diet and foraging styles of larval and juvenile fishes are sometimes mentioned as well.

SPAWNING: Spawning time and habitat, courtship behaviour and rituals, time until hatching, age at maturity and life span are discussed in this section. The information that we are able to include varies depending on the species, because for some species a lot of information is available, and for others, very little.

OTHER NAMES: Any species of fish may be known by many different names, depending on who is talking about it. The name that we use throughout the text is the name that has been accepted as the North American standard by scientists. Names change over time, though, and nicknames also form. In this section we list other names that people may use when talking about the species.

DID YOU KNOW? Here we dig a little deeper to find an interesting bit of trivia that most people do not know about a fish.

HABITAT: The habitats we have listed describe where the species is most commonly found outside the spawning season. Depending on water temperature and oxygen concentration, however, fishes may turn up in unexpected places at times.

STATUS: Definitions of all status descriptions are included in the glossary on page 166. Often, two different descriptions are given for status. The first (abundant, common, uncommon and rare) describes broadly how common the fish is in the province. The second is based on the Alberta government document *The General Status of Alberta Wild Species 2000* and identifies how much a species is at risk of endangerment, based on its rarity and threats to the species and its habitat.

RANGE MAPS: The range map for each species represents the overall range in an average year. A species is generally restricted to its preferred habitat within the highlighted range. These maps do not show small pockets within the range where a species may actually be absent or how the range may change from year to year. A possible range is denoted with a question mark.

SIZE MEASUREMENTS: Average and maximum measurements are approximate, and they are from Alberta, unless otherwise indicated. Length measurements are in total length (from the tip of the snout to the tip of the tail when both lobes of the tail are pressed inward). Fish-lovers who want to know if their prized specimen is a new record should contact the Alberta Fish and Game Association (contact information on page 171) or the University of Alberta Zoology Museum.

ID: Wherever possible we include only external characteristics so that you can identify a fish without disturbing it too much. However, some fishes cannot be told apart by only external characteristics. For example, you may have to stick your finger in a fish's mouth to feel for the presence of teeth in the base of the throat.

SIMILAR SPECIES: Easily confused species are discussed here briefly. We point out the most relevant field marks, reducing the subtle differences between species to easily identifiable traits. You may find it useful to consult this section when finalizing your identification.

KEYS TO THE FISHES

This key to the families and the family keys that follow will help you with identification as you discover all of the fishes in Alberta. The keys don't include appendix species, because those species are often rare and are usually distinctive.

Please see the Fishwatching section (p. 31) in the introduction for an overview of the best ways to view fishes. You should be able to keep a fish in water as you examine most of the features mentioned in the keys. To view a few characteristics you may need to take the fish out of water, but remember that a fish should not be out of water for any longer than you are comfortable holding your breath. Please also keep in mind that it is illegal to confine a fish that is at risk.

KEY TO THE FAMILIES

1a. No paired fins; no jaws; round toothed disc in place of mouth; seven external gill openings . . . . **lamprey family (p. 40)**

Lampetra camtschatia

round toothed disc

1b. Paired fins; jaws present; gills covered by a bony plate. 2

2a. Adipose fin present 3

adipose fin

Oncorhynchus mykiss

2b. Adipose fin absent. 7

3a.   Four pairs of barbels around mouth; no scales; large spine in each pectoral
fin . . . . **bullhead catfish family (p. 44)**
3b.   No barbels; scales present; no large spines in pectoral fins   4

4a.   Pelvic fins overlap with pectoral fins; two rows of spots along each side of
upper half of body and one row of spots along top of body . . . .
. . . . **trout-perch family (p. 47)**

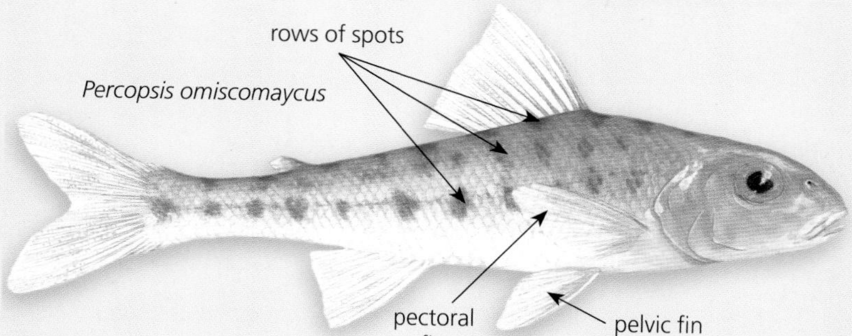

rows of spots

Percopsis omiscomaycus

pectoral
fin

pelvic fin

4b.   Pelvic fins well behind pectoral fins; spots scattered over body . . . .
. . . . **trout family (p. 44)**

7a.   One dorsal fin.   8
7b.   Two dorsal fins   13

8a.   Dorsal fin is far back on body   9

Hiodontergisus

8b.   Dorsal fin is near midsection of body   12

Notropsis hudsonius

9a. 4–11 isolated dorsal spines ahead of dorsal fin; adults rarely more than 9 cm in length . . . . **stickleback family (p. 47)**

dorsal spines

Culaea inconstans

9b. No isolated spines on back; adults larger than 9 cm in length 10

10a. Body not elongate; laterally compressed, deep body; blunt snout . . . . **mooneye family (p. 40)**
10b. Long body is fairly rounded in cross-section; long snout. 11

11a. Four barbels hang from snout; ventral, tubelike mouth; five rows of bony plates along body . . . . **sturgeon family (p. 40)**

barbels

Acipenser fulrescens

11b. No barbels; terminal mouth. . . . . **pike family (p. 44)**

Esox lucius

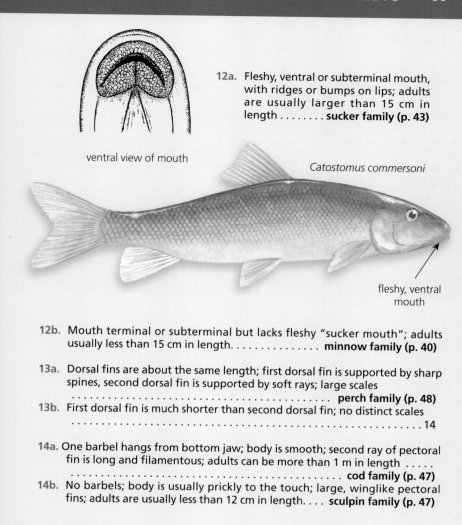

ventral view of mouth

12a. Fleshy, ventral or subterminal mouth, with ridges or bumps on lips; adults are usually larger than 15 cm in length . . . . **sucker family (p. 43)**

Catostomus commersoni

fleshy, ventral mouth

12b. Mouth terminal or subterminal but lacks fleshy "sucker mouth"; adults usually less than 15 cm in length. . . . . **minnow family (p. 40)**

13a. Dorsal fins are about the same length; first dorsal fin is supported by sharp spines, second dorsal fin is supported by soft rays; large scales
. . . . **perch family (p. 48)**

13b. First dorsal fin is much shorter than second dorsal fin; no distinct scales
. . . . 14

14a. One barbel hangs from bottom jaw; body is smooth; second ray of pectoral fin is long and filamentous; adults can be more than 1 m in length . . . . .
. . . . **cod family (p. 47)**

14b. No barbels; body is usually prickly to the touch; large, winglike pectoral fins; adults are usually less than 12 cm in length. . . . **sculpin family (p. 47)**

Cottus cognatus

large, winglike pectoral fins

LAMPREY FAMILY

Lampreys have changed very little over 400 million years. They are very different from all other fishes in Alberta. Their gill openings are uncovered (the gills of most fishes are covered by a bony operculum) and are visible as seven gill slits on each side of their bodies. Their mouths are jawless and unmistakable. Their scaleless bodies are eel-like in appearance and have only dorsal fins and caudal fins. In addition, their skeletons are composed entirely of cartilage; most fishes have bony skeletons. • Lampreys spend most of their lives as larvae called "ammocoetes," filter-feeding in the mud bottoms of freshwater streams and lakes. Adults can be parasitic, using their sucking discs to latch onto prey, or non-parasitic, ceasing to eat once they start metamorphosing into adults. Lampreys, like Pacific salmons, die after spawning.

STURGEON FAMILY

These relics of the dinosaur age are widespread throughout the northern hemisphere. Their scaleless bodies are covered with five rows of bony armour that have successfully protected them from predation for about 100 million years. Their pointed, needlelike snouts with whiskerlike barbels and their asymmetrical tails are also distinctive. • One of the most impressive features of this family is the large size and long lifespan that individuals can reach—North American species can reach lengths of over 4 m, and in Canada, sturgeons can live to over 150 years old. Only the Lake Sturgeon is found in Alberta.

MOONEYE FAMILY

There are only two species in this North American family, and they both reside in our province. These wide-eyed and deep-bodied fishes are well adapted to live in the silty waters of Alberta's large rivers. They have semi-buoyant eggs, which float close to the surface of the water instead of falling to the silty depths of the river and suffocating. Also, their eyes lack cones, the structures that allow animals to see colours. Presumably, seeing in shades of black and white is all that is necessary in the murky water that these fishes inhabit.

KEY

1a.   Top half of eye is golden, bottom half is silvery; origin of dorsal fin is in front of origin of anal fin; upper jaw doesn't extend past eye; underbelly is sharply ridged only from pelvic fin to anal fin . . . . **Mooneye (p. 56)**

1b.   Eye is completely golden; origin of dorsal fin is equal with or behind origin of anal fin; upper jaw extends past eye; underbelly is sharply ridged from pectoral fin to anal fin. . . . . **Goldeye (p. 54)**

MINNOW FAMILY

This family is the largest fish family, with over 2000 species worldwide. Of the 52 species found in Canada, 14 native species and two introduced species are present in the waters of our province. Minnows eat algae and zooplankton and, in turn, are food for many piscivorous animals. They are known for their small size (but not all minnows are small: some pikeminnows can grow to at least 1 m in length), and small individuals of any species are often mistakenly called "minnows." Minnows have Weberian ossicles—four modified vertebrae that connect the air bladder to the inner ear—which provide them with better hearing than many fishes. They also have teeth on the last gill arches in the throat instead of on their jaws. In addition, injured individuals release alarm substances that let other fishes in the school know that there is danger ahead.

KEY

1a. Visible barbel in corner of upper jaw   2
1b. No barbel or tiny, barely visible barbels   4

2a. Very subterminal mouth, with snout extending far past lower jaw . . . . . .
. . . . **Longnose Dace (p. 82)**
2b. Mouth either terminal or slightly subterminal   3

3a. Mouth terminal; upper jaw doesn't or barely extends to the front of the eye; origin of dorsal fin is equal with or slightly behind pelvic fin origin . . . . **Lake Chub (p. 58)**
3b. Mouth slightly subterminal; upper jaw extends to the front of the eye; flattened head; origin of dorsal fin is parallel with or in front of origin of pelvic fins . . . . **Flathead Chub (p. 78)**

4a. Origin of dorsal fin behind origin of pelvic fins.   5

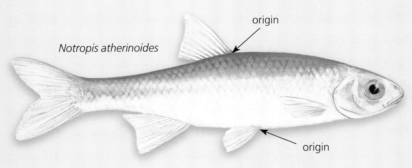

Notropis atherinoides

origin

origin

4b. Origin of dorsal fin equal with or in front of origin of pelvic fins 10

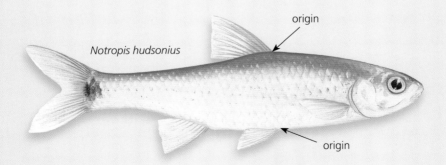

Notropis hudsonius

origin

origin

5a.   Greater than 10 anal fin rays.   6
5b.   Fewer than 9 anal fin rays   7

6a.   Up to 12 anal fin rays; iridescent silvery colour; slender bodied . . . .
. . . . **Emerald Shiner (p. 66)**
6b.   Up to 17 (rarely 22) anal fin rays; red and yellow colours on body, with
especially bright colours on breeding males; deep bodied . . . .
. . . . **Redside Shiner (p. 84)**

7a.   Mouth extends past the front of the eye   8

mouth extends
past front of eye

Margariscus margarita

7b.   Mouth does not extend to the eye   9

8a.   Up to 44 cm in length; large mouth; cone-shaped head; found only in the
main stem of the Peace River in Alberta . . . .
. . . . **Northern Pikeminnow (p. 80)**
8b.   Up to 11 cm in length; mouth is pointed down slightly . . . .
. . . . **Finescale Dace (p. 74)**

9a.   Two black lateral bands on each side; mouth is clearly pointed downward;
breeding males have red band below lower black band and have a bright
yellow belly; no barbel . . . . **Northern Redbelly Dace (p. 72)**
9b.   Single black lateral band on each side fades in adulthood; breeding males
have red band below black band and have a whitish belly; small barbel in
corners of upper jaw may be present (very difficult to see) . . . .
. . . . **Pearl Dace (p. 64)**

10a.   Scales on anterior part of body (before dorsal fin) are more crowded than
on rest of body; terminal mouth; breeding males have black heads and
prominent light-coloured nuptial tubercles on forehead . . . .
. . . . **Fathead Minnow (p. 76)**
10b.   Scales are evenly spaced over entire body; mouth is slightly subterminal
. 11

11a.   Silver-coloured body, with black spot at the base of the caudal fin . . . . . .
. . . . **Spottail Shiner (p. 70)**
11b.   Silver-coloured or brass-coloured sides, with no spot at the base of the
caudal fin 12

12a. Brassy or yellow on sides; rounded dorsal fin; dark outline on dorsal fin rays . . . . **Brassy Minnow (p. 62)**
12b. Silvery sides; fairly pointed dorsal fin 13

13a. No lateral band on body; found only in the Milk River . . . .
. . . . **Western Silvery Minnow (p. 60)**
13b. Greyish lateral band; found in the Oldman, South Saskatchewan and North Saskatchewan river drainage basins . . . . **River Shiner (p. 68)**

SUCKER FAMILY

Known as the vacuums of the fish world, suckers can survive in many different environments, as long as there is food to eat in the muck at the bottom of a water body. Both lips of their fleshy mouths are positioned on the underside of their bodies. • These fishes are good for fishwatching, because their daytime spawning runs often boast thousands of individuals. Many piscivorous animals depend on these spawning runs for food in spring and early summer. • Suckers are closely related to minnows. Like minnows, they have Weberian ossicles, have teeth on their last gill arch, and release alarm substances. However, they are generally larger than minnows and have different mouths.

KEY

1a. Long, sickle-shaped dorsal fin, with up to 30 rays; deep body with a high rise from the head to the back . . . . **Quillback (p. 86)**
1b. Short dorsal fin, with from 9–18 rays, is rectangular or triangular in shape; body is fairly round in cross-section 2

2a. Mouth has bumps and ridges or only ridges 3
2b. Mouth has only bumps 4

3a. Lips have ridges; bottom lip has a straight back edge; squared dorsal fin; caudal fin reddish orange . . . . **Shorthead Redhorse (p. 98)**
3b. Top lip has ridges and bottom lip has bumps; back edge of bottom lip is very indented (looks like a reverse "V"); rounded dorsal fin . . . .
. . . . **Silver Redhorse (p. 96)**

4a. Notches on either side of mouth where bottom lip meets upper lip . . . . .
. . . . **Mountain Sucker (p. 94)**
4b. No notch on either side of mouth. 5

5a. Small scales, usually greater than 90 along lateral line; snout of adult is relatively long (protrudes past mouth) . . . . **Longnose Sucker (p. 88)**
5b. Relatively large scales, usually fewer than 80 along lateral line; snout barely protrudes past mouth 6

6a. Dorsal fin has 13–16 rays; narrow caudal peduncle; found only in the western arm of the Peace River and its associated drainage basins . . . . .
. . . . **Largescale Sucker (p. 92)**
6b. Dorsal fin has from 11–12 rays; thick caudal peduncle . . . .
. . . . **White Sucker (p. 90)**

BULLHEAD CATFISH FAMILY

Bullhead catfishes (also known as madtom catfishes) rarely use their sense of sight when feeding (in fact, three species in this family are blind!). Instead, they rely on the eight barbels around their mouths to sense prey hiding in the mud or murky water. Species in this family were given the name "catfish" because the long barbels around their mouths reminded people of cats' whiskers. • Fishes in this family can communicate with sound that is produced with their swim bladders or their pelvic fins. They generally use these sounds during courtship and when showing aggression. • Currently, there is only one member of this family in our province. However, there is evidence that another species once roamed our rivers. The Channel Catfish (*Ictalurus punctatus*), now found in central Canada and the midwestern United States, is thought to have occurred in Alberta until about 200 years ago, based on bones found at First Nations campsites and at fur-trading posts.

PIKE FAMILY

All members of the pike family have long, rounded bodies with ducklike snouts. They are found throughout the northern hemisphere, where they prey on aquatic animals, including fishes, aquatic birds and amphibians. Their hunting strategy is to lie in wait, hidden by vegetation, until prey swims by. Their sharp jaws grab the prey in the middle and then flip the quarry around so that they can eat it head first. Fishes in this family have teeth not only on their jaws, but also on the roof of their mouths and on their tongues. • Only five species make up this family, and the Northern Pike is the only species found in our province.

TROUT FAMILY

Members of this family are commonly referred to as **salmonids** because the scientific name for the family is Salmonidae. These fishes are generally the most popular sport fishes in the northern hemisphere where they are native. They are so popular that many species have been introduced to places outside their natural range by humans. Some have even been successfully introduced to every continent except Antarctica. • This family can be broken up into three distinct subfamilies. Members of the **whitefish subfamily** are just that, silvery or whitish fishes that have large scales and few or no teeth. The **grayling subfamily** includes the Arctic Grayling, which has a distinctive large and colourful dorsal fin. The **trout subfamily**, to which the rest of the fishes in this family belong, can be further broken down into chars and true trouts. **Chars** have no dark spots on their sides and backs. **True trouts** have dark spots over at least part of their bodies.

KEY

1a.	Large scales; no or few spots on a white or silvery body	2
1b.	Small scales; dark or light spots on body; distinct teeth in mouth . . . . **trout subfamily**; go to 8	

2a.	Very large dorsal fin with red or purple spots; silver body with a few black spots concentrated near the front of the body; pelvic fins have bright orange stripes; small teeth . . . . **grayling subfamily**; go to **Arctic Grayling (p. 116)**	
2b.	Dorsal fin small; very small teeth or no teeth in mouth . . . . **whitefish subfamily**; go to 3	

3a.   Anterior ray of dorsal fin extends past the base of the posterior ray when pressed down; centre of nostril has two flaps of skin   4

Coregonus clupeaformis

3b.   Anterior ray of dorsal fin does not extend past the base of the posterior ray when pressed down; centre of nostril has one tiny flap of skin   6

Prosopium williamsoni

4a.   Subterminal mouth . . . .**Lake Whitefish (p. 108)**
4b.   Terminal or supraterminal mouth.   5

5a.   Usually 35–42 gill rakers; found only in Barrow Lakes. . . . .
. . . . **Shortjaw Cisco (p. 106)**
5b.   Usually 43 or more gill rakers . . . . **Cisco (p. 104)**

6a.   Very rounded body in cross-section; origin of pelvic fin is even with end of dorsal fin; may have brownish spots on head and adipose fin; found (so far) only in Wood Buffalo National Park . . . . . . **Round Whitefish (p. 112)**
6b.   Origin of pelvic fin behind origin of dorsal fin or parallel with middle of dorsal fin.   7

7a.   Small adipose fin; relatively large scales; rounded snout; average length 14 cm . . . . **Pygmy Whitefish (p. 110)**
7b.   Large adipose fin; somewhat pointed or bulbous snout; average length 30 cm . . . . **Mountain Whitefish (p. 114)**

8a.   No black spots; spots lighter than background colour; spots can be white to red; white edges on paired fins . . . . **char**; go to 9

8b. Black spots on a lighter background; may have some red or blue spots . . .
. . . . **true trout**; go to 11

9a. Irregular whitish spots over whole body; forked caudal fin with spots . . .
. . . . **Lake Trout (p. 130)**
9b. Pinkish to red spots among whitish spots; may have bluish haloes surrounding red spots. 10

10a. Vermiculations (wavy "worm tracks") on back, including the dorsal fin;
sides have red spots surrounded by bluish haloes . . . **Brook Trout (p. 128)**
10b. No dark markings on back and dorsal fin; no bluish haloes around spot
. . . . **Bull Trout (p. 126)**

11a. Black spots concentrated near tail; golden iridescence; may retain parr
marks into adulthood; no red slash under jaw; found only in a few southern mountain lakes . . . . **Golden Trout (p. 122)**
11b. Black spots typically cover much of the body; may also have red spots with
blue haloes. 12

12a. Large, irregular black spots and red spots surrounded by blue haloes; dorsal
fin is also spotted . . . . **Brown Trout (p. 124)**
12b. Dense, small black spots along body including head, dorsal fin and caudal
fin; pinkish iridescence 13

13a. Red slash under jaw; teeth are present on bottom of throat between gills
(basibranchial teeth) . . . . **Cutthroat Trout (p. 118)**

Oncorhynchus mykiss

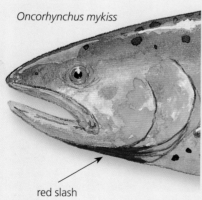

red slash

basibranchial
teeth

13b. No teeth on bottom of throat between gills; absence of red slash under
jaw, or slash may be pale orange . . . . **Rainbow Trout (p. 120)**

Note: Be aware that Cutthroat Trout and Rainbow Trout often hybridize; the
only way to really distinguish between the two species is to check for the presence or absence of basibranchial teeth (recommended only for fishes that are
already dead!).

TROUT-PERCH FAMILY

There are only two species in the trout-perch family. They have large heads, large mouths and tapering bodies, and they do not grow longer than 20 cm. The presence of both a prominent, perchlike dorsal fin and a troutlike adipose fin influenced the family name. Weak spines are present in the dorsal, anal and pelvic fins. • Canada's waters are home to the Trout-perch. The other species in this family, the Sand Roller (*Percopsis transmontana*), is found in the Columbia River basin in the northwestern United States.

COD FAMILY

The cod family is composed primarily of bottom-dwelling marine fishes, such as Atlantic Cod and Alaska Pollock, which are commercially valuable. The species in Alberta, the Burbot, is the only completely freshwater species. Some scientists have suggested that the Burbot belongs in its own family, but so far no conclusive decision has been made. Like its marine relatives, the Burbot is a benthic, coldwater species. However, unlike its relatives, which have three dorsal fins and two anal fins, the Burbot has only two dorsal fins and one anal fin.

STICKLEBACK FAMILY

Spines sprout from the backs of these charsimatic little fishes and are also present in the pelvic fins and in front of the anal fin. • Sticklebacks are popular with fishwatchers and behavioural scientists because of their involved mating and nesting rituals. Their nests are incredible structures that are glued together by a sticky kidney secretion. • The seven species in this family inhabit either saltwater or freshwater habitats or inhabit both at different times in their lives. Of the five species in Canada, three species are found in Alberta (the Threespine Stickleback is included in the appendix).

KEY

1a. 7–11 spines on back that alternate in direction, from left to right; thin caudal peduncle . . . . **Ninespine Stickleback (p. 138)**

1b. 4–7 spines on back, arranged in a straight line (not in alternating directions) . . . . **Brook Stickleback (p. 136)**

SCULPINS

Most species in this large family of bottom-dwelling fishes live within the oceans of the world. Sculpins have arrow-shaped bodies that taper from large, wide heads to skinny tails. They have large, fanlike pectoral fins and long dorsal and anal fins. The pairs of "spines" on their heads discourage predators from eating them—that is, of course, if predators can even find these well-camouflaged fishes in their rocky hiding places. • There are about 300 species in this family, eight of which are found in Canada. Four species are found in Alberta's rocky lakes and rivers.

KEY

1a. Dorsal fins are far apart, not touching; found only in Waterton Lakes . . . . **Deepwater Sculpin (p. 146)**

1b. Dorsal fins are very close or touching 2

2a. Flat, wide head in profile; upper preopercular (cheek) spine is long and curves inward toward the head; prickles cover body . . . .
. . . . **Spoonhead Sculpin (p. 144)**

Cottus ricei

preopercular
spine

2b. Head rounded in profile; upper preopercular (cheek) spine is small and somewhat curved; few prickles on body 3

3a. Teeth present on roof of mouth; found only in the Milk River and associated drainage basins . . . . **Shorthead Sculpin (p. 142)**

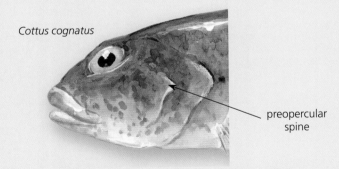

Cottus cognatus

preopercular
spine

3b. Teeth absent from roof of mouth; found only in northern Alberta
. . . . **Slimy Sculpin (p. 140)**

PERCH FAMILY

Most of the 155 species in the perch family inhabit lakes and streams in the eastern part of North America. The number of species present generally declines from east to west. • Perches are best known for having two dorsal fins, the first supported by sharp spines and the second by flexible rays. Males in this family can be very colourful during the spawning season. • There are 15 species of perch in Canada. Five members of this family occur in Alberta, and they range in size from the tiny Iowa Darter to the large Walleye.

KEY
1a. Up to 12 cm in length; caudal fin squared; mouth short, not extending to eye 2

1b. Usually more than 12 cm in length; caudal fin forked; mouth long, extending to the centre of the eye or just before 3

2a. Anal fin is smaller than second dorsal fin; first dorsal fin has 8–10 spines; snout is blunt and rounded; there may be a pink to orangish hue to fins and body. . . . . **Iowa Darter (p. 148)**

Etheostoma exile

2b. Anal fin is equal in size to second dorsal fin; first dorsal fin has 12–16 spines and rows of spots; flat head; cone-shaped snout . . . . . **Logperch (p. 150)**

Percina caprodes

3a. Deep body; thick yellow and black saddles on body; mouth extends downward to just before the eye; pelvic fin bases are very close together
. . . . **Yellow Perch (p. 152)**

3b. Slender body; mouth extends backward to the centre of the eye; pelvic fin bases are separated by a distance equal to the width of a fin 4

4a. Black and gold mottling over body; dark spot on first dorsal fin where the back end of the fin meets the body; first two rays in the first dorsal fin are smaller than the third; white tip on the bottom lobe of the caudal fin and sometimes on the anal fin. . . . . **Walleye (p. 156)**

4b. Irregular black mottling on sides and back; first dorsal fin has rows of black spots; fins are white with random dark mottling (except for the dorsal fin); no white blotch on lower lobe of caudal fin . . . . **Sauger (p. 154)**

Note: Be aware that the Walleye and Sauger can hybridize where their ranges overlap.

ARCTIC LAMPREY — *Lampetra camtschatica*

Just seven little larvae burrowed into the mud near the Slave River Rapids close to Wood Buffalo National Park in 1983 revealed to fish biologists that the ancient Arctic Lamprey was spawning just south of the Northwest Territories border. This discovery remains the only record of Arctic Lamprey in the province. • Lampreys are usually anadromous, which means they spend most of their lives in salt water and return to fresh water only to spawn. Alberta's Arctic Lamprey are part of the completely freshwater population of Great Slave Lake in the Northwest Territories. • An Arctic Lamprey spends most of its life as an ammocoete (lamprey larva) buried within the bottom substrate of a river, sucking up plankton and algae. As an ammocoete, the lamprey's eyes are underdeveloped, leaving it to rely on its mouth to find food. Metamorphosis into an adult occurs after four years. The adult lamprey emerges from the bottom sediment to prey on larger fishes, such as Lake Trout, during the last year of its life. The raspy tongue scrapes through the host fish's skin to feed on blood and other bodily fluids. Some freshwater lampreys never fully develop the sharp sucking parts of adult anadromous lampreys, disregarding food during their brief adult lives until they spawn and die. • The Arctic Lamprey's swimming technique resembles that of an eel. It may use its powerful mouth to suck onto large rocks while resting or spawning or even while making its way up difficult stretches during migration.

VIEWING TIPS: Lampreys can ascend slick rocks of waterfalls, so it is just possible that an extremely lucky fishwatcher might catch a glimpse of an Arctic Lamprey wriggling up Rapids of the Drowned, in the series of magnificent Slave River Rapids near Fort Smith, Northwest Territories. Next door to Alberta, in British Columbia, Pacific Lampreys (*Entosphenus tridentatus*) can be seen doing just that at the Morristown Canyon on the Bulkley River. In July, when the salmon are running up the Skeena River system, this easily accessible waterfall along Highway 16 (right in Morristown) is a prime fish-viewing site. Salmon work their way through the fish ladders and lampreys climb the rock and concrete walls.

FEEDING: *Ammocoete:* filter-feeds on diatoms, zooplankton and algae within the sediment. *Adult:* latches onto a large host fish to suck bodily fluids or does not eat.

SPAWNING: April to July; migrates to tributaries; 2–8 individuals create an elongated nest of small rocks by carrying the rocks with their mouths; female attaches her mouth to a steady rock or substrate; male attaches his mouth to the female's head and wraps his body around her to spawn; adults die after spawning; eggs are dark blue and hatch in three weeks; live up to four years as ammocoetes and up to one year more as adults.

OTHER NAMES: Northern Lamprey, Stone Sucker.

STATUS: very rare; undetermined status.

HABITAT: *Ammocoete:* bottom sediment of rivers and tributaries. *Adult:* large lakes and rivers.

DID YOU KNOW? The first fishes to evolve hundreds of millions of years ago were jawless. Today, out of the about 25,000 species of fishes in the world, only 38 species are jawless, and they are all lampreys.

ID: eel-like and scaleless; **seven pairs of gill openings; two dorsal fins not touching,** the first fin is flat and the second is triangular or diamond-shaped; caudal fin is spade-shaped; one central nare. *Ammocoete:* smaller version of adult; very small or non-existent eyes; fleshy hood covers mouth. *Adult:* small eyes; mouth is a circular sucking disc.

SIMILAR SPECIES: none.

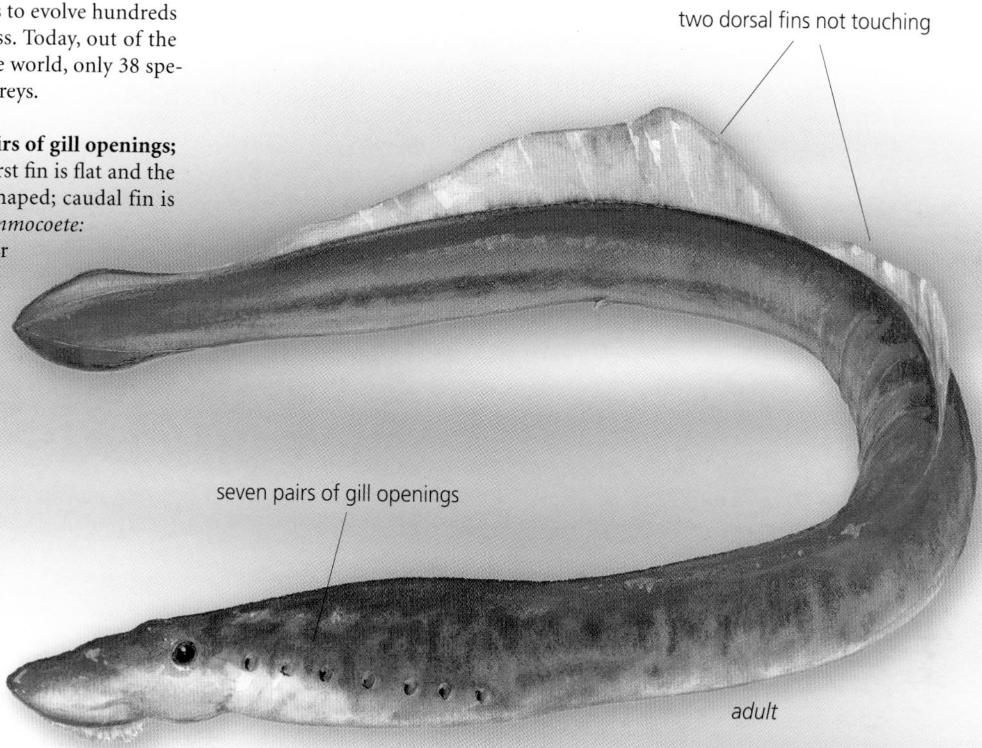

two dorsal fins not touching

adult

seven pairs of gill openings

LENGTH: *Average:* 10 cm (ammocoete); 20–30 cm (adult; Northwest Territories). *Maximum:* 15 cm (ammocoete); 63 cm (adult; Siberia).

LAKE STURGEON *Acipenser fulvescens*

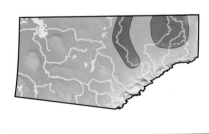

I n a province with an unfortunate lack of sea monsters, the Lake Sturgeon is an intriguing substitute. For 100 million years, this relic has nosed through sludge for its food, using the four barbels that surround its mouth to detect an assortment of benthic creatures. • Because of the five rows of hard plates called "scutes" running down its body, the scaleless Lake Sturgeon has few natural enemies. However, humans were responsible for a downfall of this species when commercial, subsistence, and sport fisheries from the late 19th century to the mid-20th century depleted the Alberta population to dangerous levels. A 28-year moratorium on harvesting Lake Sturgeon in Alberta has allowed the populations to recover, although special regulations still surround its harvest. Today, the number of adult Lake Sturgeon in Alberta is quite low, with only a few hundred older, spawning-sized fish in the North Saskatchewan and South Saskatchewan river basins. The numbers of young are in the low thousands, but populations in both of the rivers are carefully monitored and managed with concern. • Lake Sturgeon are long lived and slow to populate, with the females maturing at 20 to 25 years and the males only slightly younger at 15 to 20 years. In addition, mature females breed only every four to seven years. Therefore it is a blessing that some of these fish can live up to 80 years! With such long lives, individuals can grow to nearly 2 m, becoming Alberta's largest fish.

VIEWING TIPS: Lake Sturgeon have the unusual habit of periodically rising from their deep homes and either brashly leaping into the air or subtly poking their pointed snouts above the river surface. Pick a nice warm summer afternoon and set up a folding chair overlooking a big back eddy. The North Saskatchewan River near Rundle Park in Edmonton and the South Saskatchewan River at the forks of the Oldman River and the Bow River are some good places to try. Stay awake. If you hear a big splash like a beaver, but it's the middle of the day, you've just missed seeing a Lake Sturgeon launching out of the depths like a missile. Seeing these prehistoric creatures, especially when they quietly sneak a peek out of the water with their huge fishy eyes, is a fishwatching sight seldom forgotten.

FEEDING: benthic feeder; uses barbels as feelers to find aquatic invertebrates, crustaceans, clams, plant material and algae; barbels may have taste buds.

SPAWNING: April to June; spawns near rocky substrates in large rivers; no nest; the eggs disperse and stick to rocks or other substrates on the bottom of the river; females will release from 500,000–1,000,000 small black eggs in total over 3–4 days; eggs hatch 10 days later; males spawn once every 2–3 years, females every 4–7 years; mature at 15–25 years; live up to 80 years in Alberta (but up to 154 years in Ontario!).

STATUS: uncommon; undetermined status.

HABITAT: bottom pools of large rivers, in water from 1–10 m deep; feeds along shallow margins of these deep pools.

OTHER NAMES: Rubber Nose, Black Sturgeon, Rock Fish, Rock Sturgeon, Freshwater Sturgeon, Bony Sturgeon.

DID YOU KNOW? A jellylike substance from the swim bladder of the Lake Sturgeon was historically used to make wine, beer and jellies.

ID: very long, torpedo-like shape; **five lines of armour with spikes along body** (spikes dull with age); **asymmetrical** **caudal fin** has upper lobe larger than lower lobe; dorsal fin and pelvic fins near tail; pectoral fins close to head; tube-like ventral mouth; **four barbels hang from long snout;** brown to yellowish upper body; whitish underparts.

SIMILAR SPECIES: none.

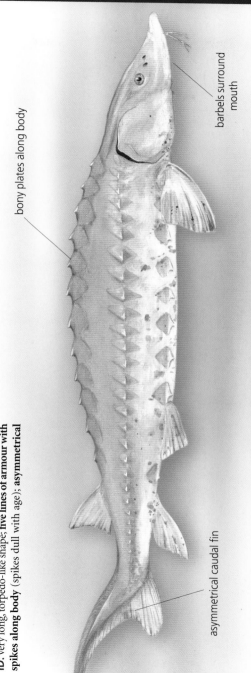

barbels surround mouth

bony plates along body

asymmetrical caudal fin

LENGTH: *Average:* 0.75–1 m. *Maximum:* 1.7 m.
WEIGHT: *Average:* 25–30 kg. *Maximum:* 48 kg.

GOLDEYE *Hiodon alosoides*

The likelihood of ever seeing the Goldeye in its silty habitat is low. Found throughout Alberta's large river systems, it prefers the muddy backwaters of river mouths. The large yellow eyes, which inspired its name, allow it to see despite the brown silt in Alberta's rivers after breakup. • Goldeye eggs are semi-buoyant, and they float safely undercover down the river until they hatch two weeks after spawning. Eggs released in Alberta most likely hatch in Saskatchewan. When an individual matures, it travels upstream, retracing its egg's path. An individual may migrate up to 2000 km in 15 days! • A mistake by a struggling entrepreneur in the 1920s led to the depletion of Goldeye in Lake Winnipeg. The young man accidentally overheated the smoked Goldeye he was trying to sell, and the flavour won the taste buds of politicians and princes around the world. "Lake Winnipeg Goldeye" has since lost much of its popularity, and some of the Goldeye that has been sold more recently actually may have come from Lake Claire in Wood Buffalo National Park.

VIEWING TIPS: River-watchers will often see evidence of Goldeye but will seldom observe the actual fish. Numerous swirls near the surface, without any fish jumping clear of the water, is a sure sign that a school of Goldeye is having a summer banquet of mayflies, stoneflies and other delectable items. Watch along the edges of back eddies in deeper parts of large prairie rivers, including the North Saskatchewan River (below the Shaw Convention Centre in Edmonton is a great site) and the Red Deer River (especially along concrete rubble shorelines in Red Deer and Drumheller, and in the deeper channels at Dinosaur Provincial Park). Calm, warm evenings in June and July are best.

FEEDING: eats zooplankton, aquatic insects, airborne insects trapped on the surface and sometimes small fishes.

SPAWNING: May to July; migrates to tributaries or upstream in its home river; spawns in slow pools and backwaters; one male per female when spawning; semi-buoyant eggs float downriver and hatch after two weeks; males mature in 6–9 years; females mature in 7–10 years; live up to 13 years.

OTHER NAMES: Winnipeg Goldeye, Northern Mooneye, Webechee, Western Goldeye, Yellow Herring, Toothed Herring, Shad Mooneye, Slicker, River Jack.

DID YOU KNOW? Goldeye are good indicators of both naturally occurring and human-introduced levels of mercury recently in a water system because they are short lived. Long-lived fishes, such as the Lake Sturgeon, can hold pollutants in their bodies for decades and are therefore not good indicators of current water body health. Goldeye showed very high levels of mercury in the 1970s, but since then the reduced industrial use of this toxin has caused mercury levels in the Goldeye population to decrease.

STATUS: common; secure.

HABITAT: large rivers and lakes with high levels of turbidity; backwaters of estuaries; wherever the bottom substrate of a water body is stirred up.

ID: square, **laterally compressed,** silver body; large scales; **large, yellow eyes; origin of dorsal fin parallel to or slightly behind origin of anal fin;** ventral keel from head to origin of anal fin; forked caudal fin. *Male:* first 10 rounded anal fin rays are longer than the rest. *Female:* first 3–4 angled anal fin rays are longer than the rest.

SIMILAR SPECIES: *Mooneye* (p. 56): only top of iris has golden hue; ventral keel is shorter (ends at base of pelvic fins); anal fin origin is farther back on body than dorsal fin origin; more rays on dorsal fin; upper jaw is shorter (does not extend as far as middle of eye).

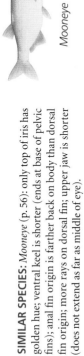

Mooneye

large, yellow eyes

origin of dorsal fin parallel or slightly behind origin of anal fin

LENGTH: *Average:* 35 cm. *Maximum:* 50 cm.
WEIGHT: *Average:* 0.75–1 kg. *Maximum:* 1.9 kg.

MOONEYE *Hiodon tergisus*

In Alberta, biologists became aware of the presence of the Mooneye in the 1970s. Its range is not as expansive as the range of its relative, the Goldeye, reaching only from the North Saskatchewan River to the South Saskatchewan River. • Many anglers mistake the Mooneye for a Goldeye. The quick way to tell the difference between the two species is to gaze into the fish's large, rounded eyes. If you see only a "half-moon" of gold at the top of the eye, the fish is a Mooneye; the iris of a Goldeye is completely golden. • The large eyes of the Mooneye allow it to feed at night, picking off invertebrates in the shallows. Unlike the Goldeye, the Mooneye does not adapt well to silty waters and prefers to stay where the rivers are relatively clear. • Mooneye mature in three to five years, with males maturing faster than females. Females, however, generally live longer than males. • One of the nicknames for this fish is "Toothed Herring" because teeth cover the Mooneye's jaws, tongue and the roof of its mouth. The species name *tergisus* means "polished" in Greek, probably referring to its shiny silver body.

VIEWING TIPS: The best places to look for Mooneye are in the North Saskatchewan River along the north bank below the Provincial Museum in Edmonton and near Duchess, Steveville and Jenner bridges over the Red Deer River. Like Goldeye, these fish are seldom seen, but fishwatchers can enjoy an evening of watching the swirls created as schools of Mooneye feed on aquatic bugs just below the river's surface. Abundant concentrations of large swirls usually indicate Goldeye, and smaller, isolated swirls are signs of Mooneye. • If you are walking along a riverside path on a summer evening and you notice plenty of mayflies or big stoneflies buzzing in the still air, quickly get yourself to the riverbank overlooking an outside bend or onto a pedestrian overpass bridge. Unlike the frenzied leaping and splashing of trouts, the more civilized and tranquil Mooneye will sedately slurp unfortunate bugs from just under the surface.

FEEDING: mostly at night in the shallows; adults eat aquatic and terrestrial invertebrates, minnows and molluscs; young eat small invertebrates and zooplankton.

SPAWNING: April to June; takes place in clear, sheltered water; 10,000–20,000 eggs are released and fall to the bottom; no nest or parental care; eggs hatch in about 14 days; mature at 3–5 years (males mature earlier than females); live to about eight years.

OTHER NAMES: Toothed Herring, River Whitefish, Shad.

DID YOU KNOW? The name of this fish's family, Hiodontidae, also means "mooneye." The Mooneye and the Goldeye are the only species in this family. In fact, these two species are the only members in Osteoglossiformes, their order, to be found in North America. The other members of this order live in tropical southern waters.

STATUS: locally abundant; secure.

HABITAT: clear waters of large rivers and their tributaries.

Goldeye

ID: square, **laterally compressed,** silver body; large scales; large eyes; **top of iris is golden and rest of iris is silver; ventral keel** between pelvic fins and anal fin; **origin of dorsal fin in front of origin of anal fin;** forked caudal fin. *Male:* rounded anal fin, first 8–10 rays are longest, with gradual decrease in ray length toward end of anal fin. *Female:* angled anal fin, first 6–8 rays are longest, with a sharp decrease in length toward end of anal fin.

SIMILAR SPECIES: *Goldeye* (p. 54): whole iris is golden; ventral keel is longer; origin of dorsal fin is equal with or behind origin of anal fin; fewer rays on dorsal fin; upper jaw is longer and extends to middle of eye.

top of iris is golden; bottom is silver

dorsal fin origin in front of anal fin origin

LENGTH: *Average:* 25–30 cm. *Maximum:* 32 cm.
WEIGHT: *Average:* 200–400 g. *Maximum:* 500 g.

LAKE CHUB *Couesius plumbeus*

The Lake Chub is one of the most widespread and northerly minnows in North America. Because it is a generalist, it can survive in almost any pool or stream in Alberta, but its preferred habitat is in water bodies with gravelly bottoms near rocky shores. As the summer heats up the shallows, the Lake Chub retreats into cooler water, making itself a good prey species for Alberta's piscivorous fishes and birds. • The male Lake Chub is one of the most persistent pursuers in the fish world, nosing the female's belly sometimes to the point where she pops out of the water. He sticks by her side, chasing away other pursuers. When she swims by a rock, he presses her against it and vibrates until she releases her eggs. • Lake Chub will mature at three or four years old, and they live only a couple more years after reaching maturity. Females grow faster yet live longer than males. • Lake Chub can be so abundant in some lakes that animals that normally aren't fish eaters can't resist chomping down on these chubby treats. Even muskrats may sit beside a lakeshore, holding onto a Lake Chub with both paws, as if the fish was a sort of silvery carrot.

VIEWING TIPS: The Lake Chub is an excellent fishwatcher's quarry. It prefers warm shallows and will often cluster near docks and walkways. Under the wooden walkway at Pyramid Lake in Jasper National Park, amazingly huge schools of Lake Chub can be seen, and Beaver River, north of Bonnyville, is another good site for viewing. • These fish grow to be some of Alberta's largest minnows, so watch carefully for some real monster chub (that's a relative term, but they can get as big as an adult's hand). • At the pulp mill near Boyle is a great display of Lake Chub in the aquarium in the main lobby. These minnows are so tolerant of environmental conditions that they can thrive in pulp mill effluent! Some of the fish in this aquarium have lived for over seven years and are quite large. • Winter is also a good viewing time for Lake Chub, because these fish can be seen readily through ice holes cut by ice fishers. Animal Lick Pond along Highway 16 in Jasper National Park near Roche Miette is a great winter site because the ice is relatively clear.

FEEDING: feeds in the shallows; eats crustaceans, zooplankton, aquatic insects, molluscs, fish larvae and algae.

SPAWNING: April to August, when water temperature is about 10° C; may migrate to tributaries or may stay near a lakeshore; male pursues a female over gravelly substrate, if available, he presses her up against a rock to initiate spawning; eggs are released in small spurts; about 10,000 eggs are released per female in a spawning season; no nest or parental care; eggs hatch in 6–20 days depending on temperature; young mature at 3–4 years old; live 5–7 years in the wild (longer in captivity).

OTHER NAMES: Creek Chub, Minnow Chub, Northern Chub, Bottlefish.

STATUS: abundant; secure.

HABITAT: almost anywhere; prefers areas with hiding places, such as large rocks.

DID YOU KNOW? The hybridization of Lake Chub with Longnose Dace has only been recorded in Alberta.

ID: terminal mouth with one small barbel at each corner of upper jaw; forked caudal fin; origin of dorsal fin parallel with or slightly behind pelvic fin origin; olive brown dorsally; silver flanks; whitish belly. *Spawning male:* a bit of red at corners of mouth; tubercles on head extend to dorsal fin; black lateral stripe; red base to pelvic fins and pectoral fins. *Spawning female:* rose colour at base of pectoral fin.

SIMILAR SPECIES: *Pearl Dace* (p. 64): barbel not visible at side of mouth; smaller mouth; spawning male has black lateral stripe above red lateral stripe.

Pearl Dace

terminal mouth with small barbel

origin of dorsal fin parallel with or slightly behind pelvic fin origin

LENGTH: *Average:* 5–9 cm. *Maximum:* 17 cm.

WESTERN SILVERY MINNOW　*Hybognathus argyritis*

Considered threatened because of its rarity in Alberta, the Western Silvery Minnow can be found only in the Milk River, near Writing-On-Stone Provincial Park. This small provincial population lives on the edge: a season of drought can dry up its much-needed pools of water. Local bottom-feeders, such as the Stonecat, are less affected by drought than Western Silvery Minnows, which inhabit the middle and surface of deep pools. When a drought does hit, these minnows abandon the dry areas, returning with the rains or snowmelt. Dams and other barriers that hinder their movements may, therefore, be an aspect of the modern world that these fish can't handle. • Outside our province, the Western Silvery Minnow spawns in weedy, slow-moving vegetation. The Milk River is slow, but lacks vegetation, so Alberta's population of Western Silveries must settle for silty, sheltered backwaters.

VIEWING TIPS: Fishwatchers should pay close attention to bright silver minnows in the backwaters of the Milk River. In addition to being a treat for the eyes, this dry-country fish may serve well as a barometer to the health of the precious low water systems in our south. The extremely low water levels in the Milk River during 2001 had Alberta fish-lovers very concerned about this prairie fish. Some parts of the Milk River had actually completely dried-up during a long drought in southern Alberta. Good news appeared, however, with the increased river flows of 2002. Biologists sampling fish along the lower stretches of the river had some of their best catches ever of Western Silveries. Where these little princesses were hiding during the drought is anyone's guess, but their recovery shows how resilient Mother Nature's residents can be to natural changes in their ecosystems.

FEEDING: eats algae, zooplankton and aquatic invertebrates.

SPAWNING: little is known about spawning; May to August; female releases up to 7000 eggs over the spawning season; young mature after first year; live to four years.

OTHER NAMES: none.

DID YOU KNOW? The Western Silvery Minnow was given the genus name *Hybognathus* because its intestine is placed on the right side of its body. In contrast, species in the *Notropis* genus have intestines on the left side of their bodies.

STATUS: rare; may be at risk.

HABITAT: turbid backwaters of rivers, usually over mud or sand.

ID: **subterminal mouth;** faint dorsal stripe; **dorsal fin origin just in front of pelvic fin origin;** brownish dorsal colour and whitish belly.

SIMILAR SPECIES: *Brassy Minnow* (p. 62): smaller on average; dorsal fin more rounded; brassy yellow on flanks. *Finescale Dace* (p. 74): distinct lateral band; terminal mouth; spawning adult has yellow underparts.

Brassy Minnow

Finescale Dace

subterminal mouth

dorsal fin origin slightly in front of pelvic fin origin

LENGTH: *Average:* 8–10 cm. *Maximum:* 11 cm.

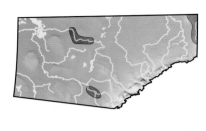

BRASSY MINNOW   *Hybognathus hankinsoni*

This metallic-looking minnow is known primarily as a Milk River resident, but it has also been discovered in both the Peace River and Athabasca River drainage basins. Fish scientists continue to be puzzled over the radically patchy distribution of this pretty minnow. In some places, it appears in tiny lakes with no connecting streams, which may be hundreds of kilometres from the next closest population. The only likely explanation is that these populations are leftovers from the great melt after the last ice age. Northern populations are more closely related to the Brassy Minnow of the Great Lakes than to their southern Alberta counterparts, which probably travelled to Canada via the Missouri River. • *Hybognathus* is Greek for "bulging jaw." The species name, *hankinsoni*, honours T.L. Hankinson, a fish biologist from North Dakota.

VIEWING TIPS: The Brassy Minnow, especially in the south, prefers silty water filled with its favourite food: algae. Small tributary streams and flood ponds created by overflowing rivers are a good place to spot a school of this species weaving in and out of the waving grasses. Brassy Minnows are easiest to spot in early spring when breeding males shine with a copper iridescence that inspired the species' name. You might have to resort to gently using a small seine net to add a sighting of these special Alberta residents to your fish list. Some great spots to try are the Milk River and its tributaries and Musreau Lake, near Grande Prairie.

FEEDING: mostly a benthic feeder; eats algae, plankton, crustaceans, aquatic insects and insect larvae.

SPAWNING: little is known about spawning; early spring; eggs hatch in one week; live to four years.

OTHER NAMES: Grass Minnow, Hankinson's Minnow.

DID YOU KNOW? If you're in an area where there should be Brassy Minnows and you find a Fathead Minnow instead, keep looking—these two species are usually found together.

STATUS: locally common; undetermined status.

HABITAT: silty, alkali water; floodplains.

ID: mouth slightly subterminal; fins rounded; **dark dorsal line;** dark line along lateral line; olive brown dorsally, fading to cream-coloured belly. *Spawning male:* brassy iridescence; may develop nuptial tubercles on pectoral fins.

SIMILAR SPECIES: *Western Silvery Minnow* (p. 60): fins more angled; more contrast between dark dorsal area and white ventral area.

Western Silvery Minnow

dark dorsal line

LENGTH: *Average:* 5–7.5 cm. *Maximum:* 9 cm.

PEARL DACE   *Margariscus margarita*

An observer may see a small, flat barbel on each side of the Pearl Dace's mouth when the mouth is held open, but occasionally the barbel is missing, so do not rely on this field mark entirely. • Look in slow, gravelly streams for males showing off the bright reddish lateral bands on their sides from autumn to late spring. During the spring spawning season females are also more colourful than usual—their undersides blush pink. In Wood Buffalo National Park, you may as well just sit back and enjoy watching these minnows instead of trying to identify them, because Lake Chub and Pearl Dace are known to hybridize there. • Fishes in the minnow family, in addition to a few other fishes such as the Iowa Darter, have skin cells that release an alarm substance when they are broken or injured. Schooling Pearl Dace react to this substance with a frenzied, chaotic getaway, followed by a few hours of hiding close to the bottom to avoid the predator that caught their school mate.

VIEWING TIPS: This charmer is found throughout Alberta, but the best viewing is in the clear streams and beaver ponds of the foothills and mountains. The beaver ponds on Shunda Creek by the small campsite west of Rocky Mountain House along Highway 11 are good places to look. Obed Lake near Hinton is also a good site. As with most minnows, a slow stealthy approach or a patient sit alongside a clear patch of calm water is your best tactic for a good sighting. If possible, plan to have the sun shining off to one side (not from your back or your front) to avoid both the sun's glare and casting a shadow across the water. • The bright orange red band across the lower side of the Pearl Dace is often unnoticed by shore-based observers. Capture with a dip net or small seine net is really necessary to fully appreciate the beauty of this fish.

FEEDING: eats zooplankton, aquatic invertebrates and algae.

SPAWNING: late spring; male defends a 20-cm-wide territory (at least 2 m away from other territories) over sand or gravel; male drives female into his area to spawn and then drives her away; both females and males spawn with more than one partner; no nest; eggs hatch in 6–20 days; adults usually live only 1–2 years but may live up to four years.

OTHER NAMES: Northern Dace, Pearl Minnow, Northern Pearl Dace.

DID YOU KNOW? A spawning male Pearl Dace will use his pectoral fins to lift the front end of a female while his caudal peduncle wraps around her back end to stretch her out. Biologists think that this position helps the female release her eggs. The nuptial tubercles on the male's pectoral fins help to grab onto the female.

STATUS: common; undetermined status.

HABITAT: small creeks with slow to moderate current; ponds and lakes; often in weedy areas or above gravel.

ID: body rounded in cross-section; **oblique, terminal mouth;** barbels may be present on either side of upper jaw; slightly mottled dorsally; silver to white on sides; white belly. *Spawning male:* orange red band below black lateral band; pectoral fins have nuptial tubercles. *Spawning female:* pink blush on undersides; female generally has smaller and shorter pectoral fins than male. *Juvenile:* distinct dark lateral line may end in a spot near caudal fin.

SIMILAR SPECIES: *Lake Chub* (p. 58): visible barbel in corner of mouth; spawning male has orange patch at base of pectoral fins. *Northern Redbelly Dace* (p. 72): smaller; no barbels; two distinct lateral bands.

Lake Chub

Northern Redbelly Dace

spawning

LENGTH: *Average:* 7–10 cm. *Maximum:* 17 cm. Females are usually larger than males.

EMERALD SHINER   *Notropis atherinoides*

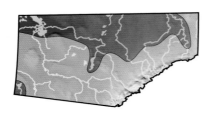

The Emerald Shiner is a very common minnow in Canada, especially in large rivers and lakes. It is an important food item for both aquatic and avian predators—pelicans, mergansers, Lake Trout and Burbot are just a few animals that feed on the Emerald Shiner. Population levels of this fish fluctuate greatly from year to year, influencing the populations of many other fishes. A lack of Emerald Shiners forces predators to prey more on other species, including some species that feed on Emerald Shiners. In turn, the drop in predators allows the Emerald Shiner population to climb, until the predator population grows so large that the numbers of these small fish drop again, and the cycle repeats itself. • These shiners spend most of their time in open water feeding on plankton. At dusk, they follow the plankton up to the surface of the water. So many Emerald Shiners can feed at one time that it may seem like rain is dimpling the water's surface.

VIEWING TIPS: This is mainly a big-lake, big-river fish, so it can be a tough sighting for shore-based fishwatchers. When Emerald Shiners come into the shallows in autumn (Ma-me-o Beach at Pigeon Lake is a good site), the best way to see them is to lean over a dock. Look for huge, dense schools of fast-moving, greyish minnows. Their bright scales reflect the sun's rays, and sporadic bright flashes, like miniature strobe lights, signal the presence of Emerald Shiners. • Late May to early June is also a good time to see these delicate minnows, as they congregate near the mouths of tributary streams or near gravel beaches to feed on the abundant fry of recently spawned suckers. • Keephills Cooling Pond, near the power plant south of Lake Wabamun, is a good winter viewing site.

FEEDING: pelagic feeder; follows rise of plankton to surface at dusk and sinking of plankton at dawn; also eats algae, fish eggs and small juveniles, worms and invertebrates.

SPAWNING: June to August; spawns over many substrates; broadcast spawner; female carries up to 3000 eggs per spawning season; eggs hatch in 24–36 hours; young mature in their second year; live up to four years.

OTHER NAMES: Lake Shiner, Common Shiner, Buckeye Shiner.

DID YOU KNOW? Emerald Shiners are a popular bait fish—schools are so numerous that people gathering these fish as bait will pickle some and sell them later on.

STATUS: common; secure.

HABITAT: lakes and large rivers; in open water most of the year; along shallow lakeshores in spring and autumn.

River Shiner

Spottail Shiner

terminal mouth

origin of dorsal fin behind origin of pelvic fin

long base to anal fin

ID: shallow, laterally compressed body; **long anal fin base with numerous rays** (usually 11); **origin of dorsal fin behind origin of pelvic fins;** large scales; cone-shaped head; **terminal mouth;** forked caudal fin; silvery overall; greenish iridescence on back and along lateral line. *Spawning male:* small nuptial tubercles on pelvic fins. *Juvenile:* somewhat transparent.

SIMILAR SPECIES: *River Shiner* (p. 68): origin of dorsal fin slightly forward of or equal with origin of pelvic fins; anal fin base shorter. *Spottail Shiner* (p. 70): dark spot on tail; origin of dorsal fin slightly forward of or equal with origin of pelvic fins.

LENGTH: *Average:* 5–7.5 cm. *Maximum:* 12 cm.

RIVER SHINER

Notropis blennius

Very little is known about the biology of this minnow in our province. The core population is found in the upper midwestern states and its distribution radiates into southern Alberta. The Alberta population of River Shiners is scattered throughout all of the large rivers that flow to Hudson Bay, although River Shiners don't actually reach the large bay. • The River Shiner prefers deep pools in large rivers, such as the South Saskatchewan, handling the spring silt loads with ease. When the amount of silt flowing down the river has decreased, River Shiners will travel to tributaries of their respective rivers to spawn.

VIEWING TIPS: It is difficult for a shore-based fish-watcher to positively identify this little shiner, especially in the often-muddy river water it prefers: time to haul out your seine net. It's actually quite a thrill to catch a River Shiner, simply because they are relatively uncommon and unknown. Some good places include the mouth of the Whitemud Creek in Edmonton and near Buffalo Bridge on Highway 886 on the Red Deer River. Pay close attention to any silvery minnow in your catch, especially

if it doesn't have a spot on its tail. Use a magnifying glass and count anal fin rays (Emerald Shiners can be confused with River Shiners, but Emeralds have a whole bunch of anal rays [usually 11], compared to seven for River Shiners). If nothing else, a seine net and a big hand lens clearly identifies you as an interesting person, and pass-ers-by will cluster about.

FEEDING: eats plankton, aquatic invertebrates and larvae.

SPAWNING: little is known about spawning; July to August; in larger creeks and tributaries over sand or gravel; probably live up to four years.

OTHER NAMES: Straw-coloured Minnow, Poor Minnow.

DID YOU KNOW? *Blennius* is derived from "blenny," the common name given to a number of ocean fishes that look like a cross between an eel and a sculpin. The River Shiner supposedly resembles a blenny, although the similarity has escaped us.

STATUS: uncommon; undetermined status.

HABITAT: large rivers; at middle to surface level of deep pools.

Emerald Shiner

ID: somewhat laterally compressed; **origin of dorsal fin parallel with or slightly in front of origin of pelvic fins;** large scales; greyish lateral band; well-developed dorsal stripe; triangular head; slightly subterminal mouth; forked caudal fin; light brown dorsally; silver flanks and belly. *Spawning male:* nuptial tubercles on pectoral fins.

SIMILAR SPECIES: *Emerald Shiner* (p. 66): long anal fin base; origin of dorsal fin behind origin of the pelvic fins; green iridescence along lateral line.

origin of dorsal fin parallel with or just in front of origin of pelvic fins

LENGTH: *Average:* 5–7.5 cm. *Maximum:* 11 cm.

SPOTTAIL SHINER *Notropis hudsonius*

Although the Spottail Shiner may not appreciate its role in aquatic ecosystems, it is an important prey species for many of Alberta's piscivorous fishes and birds. The spot near the end of its tail is important in two ways. First, the spot serves as a fake "eye," deceiving predators into attacking the tail, which allows a quick getaway. Second, it allows a fish to determine its place in the school. Schooling is an adaptation to heavy predation: individuals on the outside alert the group to the presence of a predator. Usually the older and larger fish, which have spots that have become hazy with silver over time, keep near the bottom of the school, where they are less likely to be preyed upon. • The Spottail Shiner exhibits some predatory behaviour as well; its penchant for fish eggs and larvae (even its own) has earned this fish the nickname "Spawneater." Because the Spottail eats Walleye fry, fish biologists think that it may be hindering the recovery of Walleye populations in the province. • The Spottail Shiner generally avoids the mountainous areas of the province, but its range stretches from where it was first discovered in 1893 in Medicine Hat, all the way to Alberta's northern border. • If you would like to view these shiners in the wild, you should hope for a full moon; Spottail Shiners move into the shallows of lakes and rivers at night.

VIEWING TIPS: Dock-watchers have the best chance of seeing flashing, silvery schools of Spottails. Lying on your belly, staring down into a clear lake, is both zenlike in its simplicity and ideal for relaxed observation of Spottails. As a school drifts along, you may see an individual fish cruising out of the confines of the group to snatch up a fat *Daphnia* (water flea). If a Northern Pike (or a clumsy-footed, unenlightened human dock-stomper) should approach, the school quickly closes ranks, with all fish clustered into a tight shiny mass. Spottail schools can be easily distinguished from schools of other minnows by the bright flashes of reflected sunlight as the school darts here and there. Lac La Biche, Lesser Slave Lake, Lac Ste. Anne, and Talbot Lake (wonderfully clear water for fishwatching!) and Travers Reservoir in Little Bow Provincial Park are all great places to look for these minnows.

FEEDING: feeds on plankton, aquatic and surface insects, algae and fish eggs and larvae (even of its own species).

SPAWNING: spawns over sand or gravel at the mouths of streams or rivers, sometimes in groups; female releases up to 3000 eggs per spawning season; eggs settle on the bottom; no nest or parental care; mature in first year; live up to five years.

OTHER NAMES: Spawneater.

DID YOU KNOW? The Spottail Shiner is the most northerly species of all *Notropis* fishes.

STATUS: common; secure.

HABITAT: clear rivers, streams and lakes; occasionally in silty water.

Emerald Shiner

SIMILAR SPECIES: *Emerald Shiner* (p. 66): no spot on caudal peduncle; long anal fin.

ID: dark spot at end of caudal peduncle (spot becomes silvery with age); **large scales;** slightly subterminal mouth; caudal fin forked; silver flanks with greenish yellow dorsal colouring.

spot at end of
caudal peduncle

LENGTH: *Average: 6–8 cm. Maximum: 12 cm.*

Northern Redbelly Dace

Phoxinus eos

The Northern Redbelly Dace prefers to spend its time in still waters, usually the tea-coloured acidic type in Alberta's boreal forest. This small minnow is widespread throughout the continent except west of the Rockies and is a popular bait fish. • In Upper Pierre Greys Lake, near Grande Cache, fish biologists found a curious anomaly: all of the hybrids between the Northern Redbelly Dace and Finescale Dace were female, and they composed a third of the whole population of *Phoxinus* species. Eventually they discovered that female offspring from an original meeting between a Northern Redbelly Dace and a Finescale Dace were creating clones of themselves. Female hybrids were using the sperm of spawning males only to stimulate the development of their eggs. Many unfortunate males were being tricked into thinking that their genes would continue on in the world when actually none of their genetic material was being used. Eventually, this strategy will collapse upon itself, as there will be just a pool of lonely female fish left! • Northern Redbelly Dace are found in the same habitats as Brook Trout, and usually end up as food for these trout.

VIEWING TIPS: When males are in breeding condition, which is generally all summer long, they become some of our most colourful fishes. Their bright red bellies are highlighted by black or dark olive backs and are further enhanced by startling yellow fins. These minnows can be quite abundant, but they are often difficult to see in the weedy or dark water. Easily caught with a small seine net or even by dip-netting in the shallows, they are great subjects for piscine photographers. Try foothill streams and lakes in the Hinton area, especially Upper Pierre Greys Lake. Cameron Lake, north of Stony Plain, is another good place to look for these colourful little beauties.

FEEDING: feeds mostly on algae; also takes zooplankton and aquatic invertebrates.

SPAWNING: July to August; females dart from one algae pocket to another and one or more males give chase; spawning occurs in a different algae pocket each time; eggs are non-adhesive but float inside algae; eggs hatch 8–10 days later; mature at one year, sometimes later; males live to six years, females to eight years.

OTHER NAMES: Redbelly Dace.

DID YOU KNOW? *Eos* means "dawn" in Latin, in reference to the male's sunrise-inspired spawning colours.

STATUS: locally common; sensitive.

HABITAT: small streams and boggy, calm lakes; algae must be present for spawning.

ID: two dark lateral bands; origin of dorsal fin behind origin of pelvic fins; small scales; oblique, terminal mouth; yellowish fins; forked caudal fin; dark olive brown dorsally; cream yellow underparts. *Spawning male:* **bright red belly below black lateral band;** 4–5 rows of nuptial tubercles in pectoral area.

SIMILAR SPECIES: *Finescale Dace* (p. 74): larger; only one distinct lateral band; mouth is a bit larger and less oblique; no red belly on spawning male.

Finescale Dace

oblique terminal mouth

origin of dorsal fin behind
origin of pelvic fin

♂

spawning

LENGTH: *Average:* 4–5 cm. *Maximum:* 7 cm.

FINESCALE DACE *Phoxinus neogaeus*

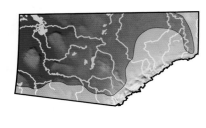

STATUS: uncommon; undetermined status.

HABITAT: slow streams; ponds and bogs of slightly higher than normal acidity.

Pockets of Finescale Dace populations are scattered throughout the province in small, boggy ponds and lakes, as well as in slow streams. These minnows may be more common than we think, and fish scientists are trying to determine if there are additional populations in the province that they don't currently know about. Finescale Dace readily hybridize with Northern Redbelly Dace and may have been overlooked in the past. • These minnows are schooling fishes, like most species in this family. When a female is ready to spawn, she breaks away from the school, zigzagging to entice a male into chasing her. Soon eager males are in hot pursuit, poking the female's abdomen with their noses. When a male has chased off other courting males, he will push or lead the female to a protected area using his pectoral fins under her belly. Walk along a pond with fallen logs or heavy vegetation in June or July, carefully lift the debris, and you may catch a couple of Finescale Dace in the act.

foothill streams seem to be the best places to spot these relatively evasive minnows. They can be found at the outflow of the beaver dams in late autumn. Perhaps they sense that the beaver pond may be too shallow for winter and are moving out to better habitat. Always check out beaver dam spillways in foothill streams, especially any water that stays ice-free during autumn or winter. These areas are great fishwatching hot spots. Tributaries of the upper McLeod River are good sites, and so is Upper Pierre Greys Lake, near Grande Cache.

FEEDING: eats crustaceans, aquatic invertebrates and algae.

SPAWNING: June to July; male clasps female with pectoral fins and caudal peduncle; female is usually braced by an object on the other side of the male; no nest or parental care; eggs are released in clumps of 30–40 during each spawning session; females may carry up to 1000 eggs; eggs hatch after one week; mature at two years; live up to six years.

OTHER NAMES: New World Minnow, Leatherback, Bronze Minnow.

DID YOU KNOW? The Finescale Dace feeds mostly on invertebrates. In turn, some bugs such as predacious diving beetles and giant water bugs feed on Finescale juveniles.

VIEWING TIPS: You'll need to capture a few of these elusive little fish with a dip net or seine net to be sure you're seeing Finescales and not Northern Redbellies. Even then, the common hybrids between these two daces could make positive identification tricky. Nonetheless, they are beautiful fish, and it is worth the effort to try to find them. Beaver ponds and

ID: body is rounded in cross-section; oblique, terminal mouth; **origin of dorsal fin is behind origin of pelvic fins;** dark olive brown dorsally; silver on flanks. *Spawning male:* **yellow band above a single dark lateral stripe;** yellowish hue to fins; nuptial tubercles on pectoral fins and occasionally on head. *Spawning female:* yellow line is similar to male's but fainter. *Juvenile:* thicker dark lateral line ends in a spot on the tail.

SIMILAR SPECIES: *Northern Redbelly Dace* (p. 72): usually has smaller mouth; spawning male has two dark bands on each side (bright red lateral stripe below dark lateral stripe).

Northern Redbelly Dace

origin of dorsal fin behind origin of pelvic fin

spawning

LENGTH: *Average:* 7 cm. *Maximum:* 9 cm.

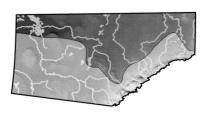

FATHEAD MINNOW   *Pimephales promelas*

Often described as the "jellybean" of the fish world, the widespread and abundant Fathead Minnow provides food for many of Alberta's piscivorous species. It is described as a "plastic" species because of its ability to adapt to changing conditions—it is sometimes the only species found in saline potholes and winterkill lakes in the prairies. • This fish is native to the interior United States and Canada, and its popularity as bait or feed for sport fishes has helped it to expand its range throughout the continent. The Fathead Minnow maintains its large population by combining frequent breeding with plenty of parental care by the male, which is a rare occurrence in the animal world. A female does not invest any effort in parenting and visits several males during the spawning season, releasing up to 10,000 eggs in three months. • The scientific name describes one of the three major characteristics of the male's breeding attire. *Promelas* is Latin for "forward black," referring to the male's dark head. During spawning, his raging hormones promote the development of a fleshy pad on his forehead. Nuptial tubercles sprout from this fleshy pad, and these tubercles remind most people of their own adolescent pimples. The male Fathead Minnow uses these nuptial tubercles to scrub his well-defended nesting site when he is preparing it for another visit from a spawning female.

VIEWING TIPS: This species is an excellent starter fish for young fishwatchers. Wade along in the warm shallows of lakes that do not have great sport fisheries (Northern Pike and Walleye eat up too many of these little minnows for good Fathead-watching). Some good lakes are Astotin Lake in Elk Island National Park, Obed Lake and Cameron Lake. Carefully watch near large rocks, chunks of logs or even, sadly, discarded beer cans and pop bottles. Daddy Fatheads are often found guarding a batch of eggs stuck to the underside of these microhabitats. Schools of nonbreeding juveniles may also scoot out of the wading fishwatcher's way, but if you stand still, these fish will usually return to nibble and tickle bare toes.

FEEDING: generalist diet includes algae, zooplankton, insect larvae and occasionally benthic organisms.

SPAWNING: midspring to late summer; in water 0.2–1 m deep; water must be over 15.6° C; eggs are released under floating or submerged vegetation (or garbage), sometimes under rock crevices; male defends a small territory and allows more than one female to spawn at a time; female spawns again in 2–16 days; male fans well-guarded eggs with his tail to increase oxygen; eggs hatch within 9–16 days; mature in the first year; live up to three years.

OTHER NAMES: Bluntnose Minnow, Hornyhead.

DID YOU KNOW? The Fathead Minnow has an extensive North American distribution, and it has also been introduced to parts of Europe.

STATUS: abundant; secure.

HABITAT: muddy pools or ditches; ponds and lakes; streams and slow rivers.

ID: thick-bodied; thick caudal peduncle; large head; **dorsal fin is black near body; origin of dorsal fin parallel to or just in front of origin of pelvic fins;** terminal mouth; dark dorsally; yellowish belly. *Spawning male:* dark head; nuptial tubercles on forehead; **dorsal pad;** thick lateral line.

SIMILAR SPECIES: *Lake Chub* (p. 58): one small barbel on each side of mouth; no dorsal pad on male. *Spottail Shiner* (p. 70): silver colour; thin, dark lateral line along smaller, thinner body; large scales; dark spot at base of tail.

Lake Chub

Spottail Shiner

nuptial tubercles

black on dorsal fin

spawning

LENGTH: *Average:* 4–8 cm. *Maximum:* 10 cm.

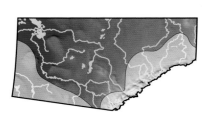

FLATHEAD CHUB *Platygobio gracilis*

This fish's scientific name describes how its body is specially designed to withstand strong currents. *Platygobio* means "broad minnow," referring to the flattened head, which gives this fish increased hydrodynamics, pushing it to the bottom of the water body where there is more shelter from currents. The second part of the scientific name seems contradictory, but *gracilis* describes the slenderness of the fish's body, which allows it to work less against the current because it displaces less water. • The Flathead Chub is most commonly found in silty water or in rivers that historically have a heavy silt load after spring break-up. Two small barbels that peek out of each side of its mouth help it to find aquatic insects within the darkened water. Anglers may find a Flathead Chub hanging on the end of their line if the fly feels similar to an aquatic insect. • A huge Flathead Chub 37 cm long was discovered in Wood Buffalo National Park in 1976 and could be a world record for the species. These minnows are one of the longest lived in their family, and their lifespan allows them to grow to these "monstrous" lengths.

VIEWING TIPS: This minnow, although very common in big rivers, is unknown to most Albertans. An angler occasionally catches one but usually mistakes it for a small whitefish. Non-angling fishwatchers may find it tough to spot one of these neat northern minnows; hanging out with an angling buddy along the North Saskatchewan, Peace or Athabasca rivers may provide the best chance of seeing a Flathead Chub.

FEEDING: uses barbels and sight to find prey; eats aquatic insects, insect larvae and terrestrial insects.

SPAWNING: July to August; travels up tributaries of larger, silty rivers; little else is known; mature at four years; live up to 10 years.

OTHER NAMES: Saskatchewan Dace.

DID YOU KNOW? The distribution of the Flathead Chub extends far north, past the town of Inuvik in the Northwest Territories.

STATUS: common; secure.

HABITAT: silty waters of large rivers and streams.

ID: slender body; **flattened head,** very little rise from head to back; subterminal mouth with one barbel on each side; **all fins sickle-shaped;** large, pointed pectoral fins; **origin of dorsal fin directly over or just in front of origin of pelvic fins;** forked caudal fin; brown yellow dorsally. *Juvenile:* dark stripe along body to end of caudal peduncle.

SIMILAR SPECIES: *Lake Chub* (p. 58): top of head more curved in profile; fins not sickle-shaped; male has orange patch at base of pectoral fin.

Lake Chub

flat head

origin of dorsal fin parallel with or just in front of pelvic fin origin

LENGTH: *Average:* 20–30 cm. *Maximum:* 37 cm.

NORTHERN PIKEMINNOW

Ptychocheilus oregonensis

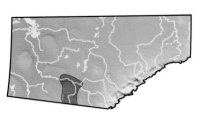

This fish's thin, flat, pikelike head inspired its current name, recently changed from the unpopular designation "Northern Squawfish." In Alberta, the Northern Pikeminnow has crossed the Continental Divide via the Peace River. Most of its range is in the West—it is very common in British Columbia and the northwestern United States. By crossing the Alberta border, this fish claimed the title of the largest minnow in Alberta, with a provincial record of 44 cm. A cousin of our Northern Pikeminnow, the Colorado Pikeminnow, can reach huge sizes of 36 kg and over 1 m long. • Juvenile Northern Pikeminnows feed mostly on invertebrates and plankton, graduating to fishes when they grow large enough. Spawning males that have the munchies may nibble on the unborn of other Northern Pikeminnows, which is most likely a strategy to increase the chances of their own progeny succeeding.

anglers). To view the Pacific Coast's ecological equivalent to Alberta's Northern Pike on its home turf, fish-lovers would best take a trip to lakes in the Smithers and Terrace area of British Columbia. In those clear, rainforest waters, you can easily see packs of this big grey predator cruising through the shallows near shore.

FEEDING: feeds mostly in the evening; piscivorous, especially in winter; in summer it also eats invertebrates and zooplankton.

SPAWNING: May to July; spawning is primarily in shallows in lakes or perhaps in slow back channels of rivers, over gravel; female is flanked by two or more males; no nest; broadcast eggs and milt over gravel; eggs hatch in one week; mature in six years; live up to 20 years.

OTHER NAMES: Columbia Squawfish, Northern Squawfish, Columbia River Dace.

DID YOU KNOW? In the Columbia River drainage basin of the United States, a bounty has been offered for pikeminnows, because they prey on the young of desired sport fishes.

VIEWING TIPS: The Peace River (upstream of the town of the same name) is the only spot in Alberta to see this fish, but its rarity and the murky water precludes viewing. It may be found on the end of an angler's line, as well as in the catch of the diligent seine-netter. Although rare and unlikely to be seen in Alberta, this giant minnow is common in the lakes of interior British Columbia (where its habit of taking bait and expensive flies has earned it the derision of some

STATUS: locally uncommon; sensitive.

HABITAT: deep pools of large rivers; young frequent shallows; usually a lake fish on western side of Continental Divide.

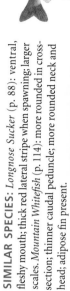

Longnose Sucker

Mountain Whitefish

ID: shallow-bodied; **cone-shaped head;** large eyes; large, **terminal mouth; origin of dorsal fin just behind pelvic fin origin;** forked caudal fin; brown dorsally; silver on sides; whitish belly. *Spawning male:* orange hue to bottom fins; white stripe below lateral line; small nuptial tubercles on pelvic, pectoral and dorsal fins and head.

SIMILAR SPECIES: *Longnose Sucker* (p. 88): ventral, fleshy mouth; thick red lateral stripe when spawning; larger scales. *Mountain Whitefish* (p. 114): more rounded in cross-section; thinner caudal peduncle; more rounded neck and head; adipose fin present.

cone-shaped head

large, terminal mouth

dorsal fin origin behind pelvic fin origin

LENGTH: *Average:* 30 cm. *Maximum:* 47 cm.
WEIGHT: *Average:* 250 g. *Maximum:* 2 kg.

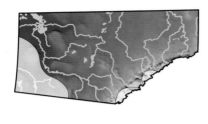

LONGNOSE DACE   *Rhinichthys cataractae*

Attempting to locate adult Longnose Dace during the day is a challenge, because these minnows spend daylight hours under rocks, hiding from predators such as Brook Trout or grebes. They emerge at night to feed on aquatic insects and insect larvae. During the day, you are more likely to see schools of juveniles as they swarm in the shallows. • Swimming close to the bottom of a fast-moving creek is relatively easy for the Longnose Dace; like most fishes that spend their time in fast water, it has a smaller swim bladder than fishes in lakes, and therefore does not need to regulate the air volume as much. • *Rhinichthys* is Latin for "snout fish," and *cataractae* refers to a waterfall, specifically Niagara Falls, where the Longnose Dace was first discovered.

Marx beak with a black moustache and a big grin. Some of the best Longnose-chasing sites are near Devon along the North Saskatchewan River and at the Red Deer River, right in the city. However, you can find these dace almost anywhere in the upper parts of most of Alberta's clearer rivers.

VIEWING TIPS: It is a lot of fun wading in the gravelly shallows, just chasing around Longnoses with little aquarium dip nets in the late summer when the rivers start to clear up and the water is low and warm. These fish are fast and know the rocky hiding places well, so it isn't as easy as you'd first think. If you are lucky enough that a Longnose will allow itself to be caught, you should put it into a pail or plastic dishpan, admire it for a few moments, and then quickly return it to its home. The young dace have the cutest little faces of any of our minnows, sort of a Groucho

FEEDING: nocturnal; eats aquatic insects, larvae, worms, molluscs, crustaceans and fish eggs.

SPAWNING: May to August; mostly in streams and some lakes; over gravel or rocks; male defends a small territory and invites female by quivering body at a sharp angle; female releases over 9000 transparent, adhesive eggs; no parental care; mature at age two; live up to six years.

OTHER NAMES: Stream Shooter.

DID YOU KNOW? The Banff Longnose Dace was a subspecies of the Longnose Dace, and is now believed to be extinct. It resided exclusively in the marshes leading to the Cave and Basin Hotsprings in Banff. Biologists think that competition with introduced tropical fishes and changes to flows and water levels in the area are responsible for the extinction of the subspecies.

STATUS: common; secure.

HABITAT: fast flowing, cold streams and cold lakes; near the bottom.

ID: shallow-bodied; **cone-shaped head;** large eyes; **large, subterminal mouth;** barbels in corner of upper jaw; **origin of dorsal fin slightly behind pelvic fin origin;** forked caudal fin; grey brown dorsally; silver on sides; whitish belly. *Spawning male:* orange hue to bottom fins; white stripe below lateral line; small nuptial tubercles on pelvic, pectoral and dorsal fins and head.

SIMILAR SPECIES: *Lake Chub* (p. 58): larger, terminal mouth with continuous groove across upper lip; barbel in one corner of mouth; spawning male has orange patch at base of pectoral fins.

Lake Chub

large, subterminal mouth

origin of dorsal fin slightly behind pelvic fin origin

LENGTH: *Average:* 5–9 cm. *Maximum:* 14 cm.

REDSIDE SHINER   *Richardsonius balteatus*

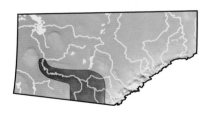

In June, water bodies in the western leg of the Peace River drainage basin sparkle yellow and red as male Redside Shiners zip about to attract females. In British Columbia, Redside Shiners are more common in lakes than rivers. They are found in only one lake in Alberta, Lee Lake near Pincher Creek, and they are only found here because of an illegal release. Luckily for our trout population, the lake is landlocked in the southwest of the province, and biologists are attempting to eliminate this unwanted and unnatural population. This little shiner can inhibit trout populations wherever it goes; it has the same invertebrate diet and will also eat the juvenile trouts. Larger trouts will in turn eat Redside Shiners, but there are usually more shiners than trouts. • Although they reside in different types of water bodies, Redside Shiners are schooling minnows, swimming near vegetation during the day and moving to deeper water at night.

VIEWING TIPS: While not commonly found in Alberta, this distinctive minnow can be very abundant in local patches in the upper Peace River system. The water in the large river is often so murky that viewing is limited. Try the clearer tributaries, such as the Little Smoky and the Wapiti. • As with a few other Pacific drainage fishes, this minnow

is best seen across the border in British Columbia. In some clear lakes in the Kamloops and Prince George area, massive schools of Redsides may surround your boat. These unmistakable fish can be caught using a tiny hook, and their deep, narrow bodies are very distinctive amongst our often-confusing minnow species. Take a few moments to appreciate these beauties, and then return them to their school.

FEEDING: feeds on invertebrates, plankton, molluscs, fish eggs and small fishes, even of its own species.

SPAWNING: June to August; males migrate first up tributaries, females arrive a few days later; female is flanked by one or two males over submerged vegetation; eggs adhere to vegetation and are covered by milt from the males; females can produce up to 3000 eggs but will release 10–20 per spawning session; eggs hatch after 15 days; mature at three years; live up to five or maybe seven years.

OTHER NAMES: Red-sided Shiner.

DID YOU KNOW? The species that most inhibits the growth of Redside Shiner populations is the Redside Shiner itself. Adults will prey upon eggs of their own species, taking a large chunk out of the population.

STATUS: locally common; secure.

HABITAT: large rivers and tributaries in Alberta; lakes in the rest of its range; requires vegetation for cover during the day.

ID: deep body; small scales; keeled along belly between pectoral and anal fins; **dark stripe through eye**; dark lateral line; pectoral fins longer on male; **large anal fin** (from 17–22 rays); **origin of dorsal fin far behind origin of pelvic fins**; deeply forked caudal fin; dark brown dorsally, fading to yellow underneath. *Spawning male:* bright yellow and red bands along sides and belly; nuptial tubercles on head and paired fins.

SIMILAR SPECIES: *Lake Chub* (p. 58): barbels at corners of mouth; anal fin with fewer rays; origin of dorsal fin just behind or equal with pelvic fins; caudal fin less forked; shallower body shape.

Lake Chub

dark stripe through eye

dorsal fin origin behind pelvic fin origin

large anal fin

spawning

LENGTH: *Average:* 10 cm. *Maximum:* 12 cm.

QUILLBACK *Carpiodes cyprinus*

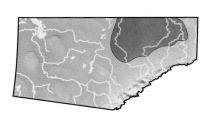

The telltale sicklelike dorsal fin of this sucker makes it easy to identify. In Alberta, the Quillback prefers warmer waters, inhabiting the North Saskatchewan River and areas south of it. • Schools of juvenile Quillbacks may expose themselves to predators when they frequent the shallows of rivers such as the Red Deer River. If they manage to avoid getting eaten by birds and other fishes, Quillbacks may live up to 12 years. • *Carpiodes* implies this species' similarity to carp, and so does *cyprinus*, which is the name of a carp genus (Cyprus is the location where the Romans first encountered carp). • The Quillback enjoys nosing through river ooze for invertebrates. It likes chewy stuff so much that anglers wishing to catch a Quillback can do so by putting a ball of dough on their hook.

Provincial Park and the North Saskatchewan River near Edmonton. If you see one, the sweeping dorsal fin should be a dead giveaway. Check at the mouths of small tributary streams in May and June. Focus your efforts in mid-summer on the deeper pools of warm, murky, grassland rivers.

FEEDING: benthic feeder; eats aquatic invertebrates, worms, molluscs, crustaceans and detritus.

SPAWNING: little is known about spawning; probably spawns in midspring; broadcast spawner; no parental care; mature at about four years; live up to 12 years (and probably older).

OTHER NAMES: Quillback Carpsucker, Long-finned Sucker, Silvery Carp, White Carp.

DID YOU KNOW? This fish is so rare in Alberta that when it is caught most folks haven't the faintest idea what it is, so they call it anything from a Goldeye to a goldfish.

VIEWING TIPS: Amongst hard-core Alberta fish aficionados, sighting or catching a Quillback guarantees instant fame. (Okay, so it's fame in a tiny group of fanatics, but it's still fame...) You'll need a healthy dose of good luck to see this rare and then likely misidentified prairie dweller in Alberta. Try the Red Deer River around Dinosaur

STATUS: rare; undetermined status.

HABITAT: large, silty rivers with slow to moderate current.

subterminal mouth

large, sickle-shaped
dorsal fin

Goldeye

Silver Redhorse

ID: **deep-bodied** and laterally compressed; **large, sickle-shaped dorsal fin with long base;** large scales; small, rounded head; fleshy, subterminal mouth; forked caudal fin; brownish above; tan on sides; whitish below; silver iridescence on body. *Spawning male:* nuptial tubercles on head. *Spawning female:* very small nuptial tubercles close to head.

SIMILAR SPECIES: *Goldeye* (p. 54): small triangular dorsal fin far back on body; iris of eye is golden; mouth is terminal; keeled anal fin; smaller scales. *Silver Redhorse* (p. 96): red fins; small, triangular dorsal fin; head is more conical.

LENGTH: *Average:* 40–50 cm. *Maximum:* 56 cm.

LONGNOSE SUCKER   *Catostomus catostomus*

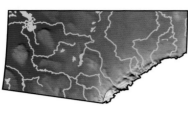

The Longnose Sucker's scientific name reinforces the obvious: *catostomus* means "inferior mouth" in Latin. The term "inferior" does not imply that the mouth has any drawbacks, only that it is on the underside of the body. In fact, the sucker mouth is one of the best adaptations for feeding from a lake or river bottom. All suckers are born with terminal mouths, and as they mature the mouths "wander" to settle underneath their snouts. The Longnose's mouth has a little farther to go than that of most suckers—as its name suggests, the nose of this sucker protrudes more than its relatives' noses in adulthood. Longnose Suckers will eat molluscs, and some people may think this poses a problem for the fleshy-lipped fish. But inside the mouth are pharyngeal teeth, which crunch up mollusc shells for digestion.

• These suckers are known to prefer cold water bodies, but Longnoses are widespread across Alberta, occurring in both lakes and rivers from the mountains to the prairies. From late May to early June, these suckers advance in large numbers up tributaries to spawn. Migration to their birth streams occurs mostly at night, but spawning takes place during the day. Males develop a bright red lateral stripe at this time, which attracts mates but also serves as a beacon for predators such as osprey. The threat of death necessitates speedy and strategic mating; both males and females spawn with more than one mate, and some will spawn an average of 40 times per hour!

VIEWING TIPS: The Longnose Sucker is one of Alberta's most commonly observed and strikingly beautiful fishes. In spring, when small streams swell with snowmelt, Longnose Suckers come out of the larger rivers and lakes for their annual spawning. Some good places to look for these beauties are the Whitemud Creek in Edmonton at the junction with the North Saskatchewan River, the Athabasca River in Jasper National Park near the bridge below the Jasper townsite and Lesser Slave Lake. Watch where streams riffle over a shallow rocky area or where a beaver dam has created a little brushy waterfall. Longnoses splash through these areas and rest in the slightly deeper holes nearby.

FEEDING: benthic feeder; eats molluscs, worms, crustaceans, detritus and aquatic insect larvae.

SPAWNING: May to July; spawns in shallow tributaries and in gravelly shallows of lakes; females are flanked by 4–5 males who take turns mating with her; a male clasps the female's pelvic or anal fins; white eggs stick to gravel; no nest; eggs hatch after 14 days; mature at 5–10 years; live up to 20 years.

OTHER NAMES: Red Sucker, Black Sucker, Red-sided Sucker, Finescale Sucker.

DID YOU KNOW? Alberta has the only record of hybridization between Longnose Suckers and White Suckers. This

STATUS: common; secure.

HABITAT: prefers cold lakes or rivers but may be found in warmer waters.

anomaly occurs in the Upper Kananaskis Reservoir and Abraham Lake. Hybridization probably occurs because of the fluctuation of water in the dammed reservoirs—variations in water level bring the deeper-spawning Longnose Suckers into the same habitat as the shallower-spawning White Suckers.

ID: large, rounded anal fin; small scales, especially toward tail; adult has **long snout;** mouth covered with bumps (papillae); slate grey or olive dorsally; white ventrally. *Spawning male:* thick, bright red lateral stripe above a black stripe; darkened back. *Spawning female:* reddish wash along sides.

SIMILAR SPECIES: *White Sucker* (p. 90): mouth closer to end of nose; larger scales, especially toward tail; no red lateral band on spawning males. *Mountain Sucker* (p. 94): mouth closer to end of nose; notch on sides of jaws; shallow cleft in lower lip; cartilaginous scraper on lower jaw.

White Sucker

Mountain Sucker

long snout

spawning

♀

large, rounded anal fin

LENGTH: *Average:* 30–50 cm. *Maximum:* 55 cm.
WEIGHT: *Average:* 1 kg. *Maximum:* 1.8 kg.

WHITE SUCKER   *Catostomus commersoni*

The White Sucker is a generalist species, able to live in habitats ranging from cold streams to warm, even polluted waters. The White Sucker is also not picky when choosing its spawning habitat; it may migrate to a stream or just to a shallow lakeshore. People who choose to camp next to one of these areas may wake in the middle of the night to the splashing and jostling of hundreds of mating White Suckers. Northern Pike, eagles, bears and other animals depend on White Sucker spawning runs for food. White Sucker fry may be a critical item in the diet of young Walleye, contrary to the popular opinion that suckers eat all the Walleye eggs. In the past, streams were so thick with spawning White Suckers that Canadian pig farmers could pitchfork loads of these fish to feed their livestock. *Commersoni* is derived from the name of an 18th-century French naturalist, Philibert Commerson, who explored much of the southern hemisphere for King Louis XV.

VIEWING TIPS: Going out in an Alberta spring to watch White Suckers is a wonderful experience. The weather is warm, the grebes are calling, and the mosquitoes haven't hatched just yet. If there has been any snowmelt of note, find a creek or river flowing into almost any big Alberta lake. The stream in the campground at Touchwood Lake, where the Sturgeon River leaves Lac Ste. Anne, and on the northwestern shore of Pigeon Lake at Tide Creek are good places to look. Check near gravelly patches (under road bridges are good spots) or at the spillways over beaver dams.

White Suckers will be moving in very shallow water, even in the bright daylight. If it's peak spawning time, you'll see splashes of water thrown up by clusters of vibrating, egg-laying fish. It's a good place to take the kids and teach them about Nature ("You see, when a Daddy fish loves a Mommy fish …").

FEEDING: bottom-feeder; mostly active at dawn and dusk; eats molluscs, crustaceans, insect larvae and algae.

SPAWNING: May to July depending on elevation and temperature; migrates to shallow lakeshores or smaller tributaries; will spawn in clear or turbid waters; prefers to spawn over gravel; takes place at dusk and dawn (and in the day when spawning is at its peak); 2–4 males flank a female, and eggs and milt are released; no nest, but individuals spawning in lakes may clean the gravel; spawning is very frequent over a period of two weeks; eggs hatch after 8–11 days; young remain at hatching site for 14 days; mature in 6–9 years; males mature one year earlier than females; usually live 10–12 years but may live to 20 years.

OTHER NAMES: Common Sucker, Eastern Sucker, Mud Sucker.

DID YOU KNOW? A hermaphroditic White Sucker (an individual with both male and female reproductive parts) was found in the Athabasca River in the 1970s.

STATUS: common; secure.

HABITAT: almost anywhere; streams, rivers and lakes; feed in shallow areas.

ID: rounded body, especially toward head; **cone-shaped head; large scales;** fleshy mouth is covered with bumps (papillae). *Spawning male:* nuptial tubercles on head and belly, but mostly concentrated on anal fin area and caudal peduncle; flanks turn golden or even display a red band; darker dorsally. *Juvenile:* 3–4 dark splotches on flanks.

SIMILAR SPECIES: *Longnose Sucker* (p. 88): snout longer; scales smaller; has red and black bands along lateral line during spawning. *Largescale Sucker* (p. 92): body more narrow; found only in the Peace River drainage basin.

Longnose Sucker

Largescale Sucker

cone-shaped head

LENGTH: *Average:* 30–50 cm. *Maximum:* 58 cm.
WEIGHT: *Average:* 1 kg. *Maximum:* 2.1 kg.

LARGESCALE SUCKER   *Catostomus macrocheilus*

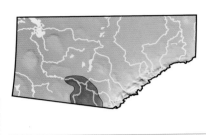

The Largescale Sucker is one of three species that have crossed into Alberta from British Columbia via the Peace River. Only juveniles have been found in Alberta, implying that the young Largescale Suckers may be crossing the border from breeding populations in British Columbia. Largescales are native to the Pacific Northwest and roam throughout the Columbia, Fraser and Peace river systems. In Alberta, they occur only in the slower-moving portions of the Peace River and its tributaries, but they are found in lakes as well as rivers in the western part of their range. • The young, with their terminal mouths, feed upon zooplankton at the edges of the river until they become bottom dwellers as adults. When grown, these suckers feed on benthic aquatic invertebrates and detritus with their fleshy, ventral mouths. The young probably serve as one of the many forage species for predaceous fishes and birds as well as bears and other mammals.

VIEWING TIPS: This fish is a rarity where it is found in the dark, silty waters of the Peace River. Fishwatchers are pretty much out of luck when it comes to seeing Alberta

Largescales. Keen fish-lovers will head for the other side of the Rockies and check out small, clear mountain streams (the areas around the towns of Valemont and McBride are nearby possibilities) just before the big snowmelt in May or June. Largescales become a beautiful pale golden colour during spawning, with a very subtle green stripe along their sides. They spawn in the daylight in very shallow water, making for easy, comfortable viewing.

FEEDING: *Juvenile:* pelagic feeder; eats zooplankton and small invertebrates. *Adult:* benthic feeder; eats invertebrates and detritus.

SPAWNING: does not spawn in Alberta.

OTHER NAMES: Coarsescale Sucker.

DID YOU KNOW? Sensitive papillae cover the mouths of most suckers, including the Largescale Sucker. These little bumps serve as "feelers" for food, similar to the barbels of other fishes such as the Stonecat.

STATUS: rare; sensitive owing to rarity in the province.

HABITAT: large rivers and streams with moderate current; deep pools with sand and gravel.

ID: oval-shaped in cross-section; **scales larger nearing tail;** slightly raised "ridge" along back behind head; forked caudal fin; mouth covered in bumps (papillae); **contrast between dark dorsal area and white underparts.** *Juvenile:* three dark lateral marks on flanks.

SIMILAR SPECIES: *White Sucker* (p. 90): body more rounded in cross-section; snout more rounded; scales smaller and of uniform size; juveniles are difficult to distinguish from juveniles of other suckers.

White Sucker

scales larger nearing tail

adult

LENGTH: *Average:* 10 cm (juvenile). *Maximum:* 60 cm (adult; British Columbia).

MOUNTAIN SUCKER *Catostomus platyrhynchus*

Very little is known about this diminutive sucker that scrapes algae from the rocks of rivers such as the North Saskatchewan and the Oldman. The little that we do know could make this species a "poster fish" for the protection of streamside habitat. The presence of streamside vegetation reduces erosion of the river banks, lessening the amount of silt in the river. It is important that silt levels remain low to maintain the flow of oxygen-rich water over the eggs. Juvenile fish also rely on vegetation for cover as they make their way from smaller tributaries to the river where they will spend their adult life. • These janitors of the watery world are important to the river ecosystem because they keep algae at bay; they may even turn upside down or sideways to scrape off the underside of boulders with the cartilaginous sheath on their jaws. • The Mountain Sucker's mouth differs from the mouth of other Alberta suckers because it has a notch on each side where the upper lip meets the bottom lip; look carefully and you can see that the bottom lip looks similar to a whale's tail.

VIEWING TIPS: The best place to look for this sucker is in the upper Milk and Oldman rivers and their tributaries and in creeks flowing into Abraham Lake (alongside Highway 11 west of Rocky Mountain House). The Mountain Sucker seldom gets bigger than the span of your hand, and spawners can be about the size of a chocolate bar. Fishwatchers can easily mistake Mountain Suckers for big minnows, so take

care in those southern Alberta foothill streams. It's hard to positively identify a Mountain from a White or Longnose sucker without catching one and checking out the pelvic fins or lips. If you don't want to get right in there with a dip net or seine net, it's probably best to just fib a bit and tell your friends that any small sucker you saw in the foothills of southern Alberta *might* have been a Mountain Sucker.

FEEDING: eats mostly the algae on boulders; occasionally feeds on invertebrates.

SPAWNING: June to July; migrates to clear tributaries; spawning occurs in riffles, sometimes beneath deep pools; females may carry up to 3000 eggs per spawning season; no nest or parental care; eggs stick to the bottom; after spawning, small schools of parents will spend time in deep pools before migrating back to the larger river; eggs hatch after 8–14 days; young remain in pools or under streamside vegetation for cover from predators; mature at 3–5 years; males live up to seven years; females live up to nine years.

OTHER NAMES: Plains Mountain Sucker, Northern Mountain Sucker.

DID YOU KNOW? The Mountain Sucker was one of the fishes collected by Lewis and Clark in Montana in 1805, but no one paid enough attention to identify this tiny fish for nearly 100 years after it was captured.

STATUS: locally common; secure.

HABITAT: mountain streams and large rivers; prefers sandy or gravelly bottoms with boulders.

ID: rounded snout; **notches where upper lip meets bottom lip,** cleft in bottom lip is small; bottom half of upper lip and bottom lip are covered in bumps (papillae); **dorsal fin is higher than the length of its base;** has tiny, bony projection at base of pelvic fin; brown with dark splotches dorsally; yellowish sides; white belly. *Spawning:* nuptial tubercles on bottom fins and bottom of caudal peduncle (more pronounced on male); male has bright red stripe above dark lateral stripe.

SIMILAR SPECIES: *Longnose Sucker* (p. 88): lips continuous; deep cleft in lower lip; lacks bony projection at base of pelvic fins. *White Sucker* (p. 90): large scales; lips continuous; deep cleft in lower lip; lacks bony projection at base of pelvic fins.

Longnose Sucker

White Sucker

bony projection at base of pelvic fin

spawning

LENGTH: *Average:* 13–17 cm. *Maximum:* 22 cm.
WEIGHT: *Average:* 50–150 g. *Maximum:* 200 g.

SILVER REDHORSE   *Moxostoma anisurum*

The Silver Redhorse has more of a bronze iridescence than a silver shine on its body—the silver in the name comes from the colour of its fins. • Throughout its eastern range this sucker can be found in both lakes and rivers, but it seems to prefer the habitat of only the North Saskatchewan and South Saskatchewan rivers in Alberta. The Silver Redhorse hangs out in the main stem of the big rivers. It favours clear water but will endure somewhat silty waters, even during spawning. • The Silver Redhorse is rare in Alberta, so look closely to make sure you are not looking at a Shorthead Redhorse. The sharp caudal fin of the Shorthead can be a helpful characteristic. Also, the Silver Redhorse has a deeply cleft (V-shaped) lower lip, and the Shorthead Redhorse has a straight back edge to the lower lip (no cleft). • *Anisurum* means "unequal tail"; the caudal fins of the two *Moxostoma* species in Alberta have a slightly smaller, sharper upper lobe.

VIEWING TIPS: You're unlikely to see this fish in its natural habitat (deeper water of murky rivers), but it is a fish worth searching out. Non-angling fishwatchers have the best chance of seeing a Silver Redhorse if they hang out with an angler buddy, especially on the North Saskatchewan River (in big pools throughout the Edmonton area), the Sturgeon River (from the mouth of the river to the Genesee Bridge) and the South Saskatchewan River around Medicine Hat. The power and fight of these fish at the end of the fishing line can lead a person to believe that they have surely caught a large sport fish. Capturing one of these beautiful, metallic-tinted fish can be the highlight of a trip.

FEEDING: benthic feeder; eats molluscs, crustaceans and other invertebrates and detritus.

SPAWNING: May to June; in shallow, silty water; male arrives first to establish a territory; female enters the territory to spawn; she releases 10,000–20,000 eggs per spawning season; mature in about five years; females can live up to 20 years.

OTHER NAMES: Silver Mullet, Whitenosed Sucker.

DID YOU KNOW? *Moxostoma* suckers (redhorses) have three-chambered swim bladders, whereas *Catostomus* suckers have two-chambered swim bladders. This characteristic could be associated with the fact that redhorses spend their time in deeper waters than other suckers.

STATUS: rare; undetermined status.

HABITAT: deep pools in large, slow rivers; prefers relatively clear water near overhanging banks.

Shorthead Redhorse

ID: slender body; **large scales;** cone-shaped head; long snout; bottom lip is V-shaped and covered in bumps (papillae); upper lip has ridges (striations); forked caudal fin; **large dorsal fin;** brown dorsally; tan flanks; white underparts; bronze iridescence over whole body; fins are silvery. *Spawning:* bronze iridescence intensifies. *Spawning male:* nuptial tubercles on anal fin and caudal fin. *Juvenile:* three dark, lateral splotches; sharper edge to dorsal fin.

SIMILAR SPECIES: *Shorthead Redhorse* (p. 98): lower lips not V-shaped (straight across the back); red fins.

large dorsal fin

LENGTH: *Average:* 40–50 cm. *Maximum:* 64 cm.
WEIGHT: *Average:* 1.5–2.5 kg. *Maximum:* 3.7 kg.

SHORTHEAD REDHORSE *Moxostoma macrolepidotum*

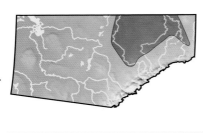

The common and scientific names of the Shorthead Redhorse point out characteristics that can help make identification easy. This short-headed fish has reddish fins, and the caudal tail, in particular, turns bright red during spawning. *Moxostoma* is Greek for "sucker mouth" and *macrolepidotum* describes this species' very large scales. What aids identification even further is that the Shorthead Redhorse has only been found in the larger rivers of Alberta, from the North Saskatchewan to the South Saskatchewan. • Unlike some suckers, this redhorse eats very little detritus. It noses through the muck at the bottom of rivers for delicious invertebrates, and will occasionally lift up off the bottom, likely chasing an enticing stonefly larva. • The Shorthead Redhorse is very sensitive to silty water and remains in less muddy tributaries when the larger rivers break in spring. However, it can endure warmer waters than many fishes and is sometimes found in unshaded, moderately fast streams.

VIEWING TIPS: Although observed less often than the White Sucker or Longnose Sucker, the Shorthead Redhorse is a real beauty for riverside fishwatchers. Two good sites are the North Saskatchewan River near Devon at Prospector's Point and the Red Deer River at Steveville Bridge, near the boundary of Dinosaur Provincial Park. Sit alongside a moderately deep back eddy that comes very near to a steep shoreline. The lucky fishwatcher will catch a glimpse of a mirror-bright, silvery green fish with a stunningly attractive red tail. In its full spawning regalia, this redhorse is our most lovely sucker.

FEEDING: benthic feeder; eats aquatic invertebrates, such as worms and molluscs; sometimes takes detritus.

SPAWNING: males migrate to primary tributaries beginning in May; males defend a small area that has a gravel or rock bottom; when a female enters the area, usually two males flank her; she may release up to 45,000 eggs; fertilized eggs scatter and settle to the bottom; no nest or parental care; eggs hatch in 7–10 days; mature at 4–5 years; live up to 14 years.

OTHER NAMES: Northern Redhorse, Common Redhorse, Redfin Sucker, Bigscale Sucker, Common Mullet, River Sucker.

DID YOU KNOW? When Shorthead Redhorses and Longnose Suckers spawn in the muddy waters of springtime, flashes of their bright red fins and sides can cause mistaken reports of Sockeye Salmon spawning in Alberta's rivers and creeks!

STATUS: common; secure.

HABITAT: clear waters of large rivers and their direct tributaries.

Silver Redhorse

ID: slender body; **reddish fins; large scales;** cone-shaped head; subterminal, fleshy mouth; lower jaw almost straight across bottom and has ridges (striations); **dorsal fin pointed and indented;** forked caudal fin; brown or olive dorsally, fading to white on ventral side. *Spawning:* caudal fin is reddish.

SIMILAR SPECIES: *Silver Redhorse* (p. 96): rounded dorsal fin; fins olive-coloured; lower lip is V-shaped; snout is slightly longer.

dorsal fin high and angled

spawning

LENGTH: *Average:* 30 cm. *Maximum:* 45 cm.

STONECAT *Noturus flavus*

Aside from getting your fingers stuck in the mouth of a Northern Pike, being stung by the Stonecat is the only pain that an Alberta fish can inflict on you. The Stonecat is the largest member of the "madtom" group of catfish, notorious for their stinging pectoral fins. A poison gland at the base of the first few spines on this fin delivers a wasplike sting if the fish is not handled properly. • Alberta's only catfish resides quietly among the rocks and riffles of the Milk River drainage basin. Perhaps this fish's affinity for hiding around boulders during the day is the reason for its name. • The Stonecat is mostly a "feeler feeder," using its eight barbels to sense benthic creatures, such as aquatic insect larvae. Stonecats feed mostly at night, and their sense of sight is rarely used in feeding. In fact, three members of the madtom family are completely blind, relying entirely on their barbels to find food. • Stonecats, like other catfishes, do not have scales—they have a smooth skin.

VIEWING TIPS: Sighting Alberta's only catfish marks a special day in the diary of any Alberta fishwatcher. Carefully wade along the warm shallows in the Milk River, watching for big brown "tadpoles" amongst fist-sized rocks. Don't disturb the fish, because they are quite likely adults guarding their eggs, which are stuck to the underside of a rock. Take care in your identification, because sculpins and baby Burbot can be easily mistaken for these little madtoms.

FEEDING: uses barbels to locate aquatic insect larvae, especially stonefly, caddisfly and midge larvae; occasionally eats small fishes, fish eggs, detritus and plant material.

SPAWNING: late spring to summer; female spawns with a single male; she deposits about 500 eggs in a gelatinous clump under a large rock or log; one parent, usually the male, guards the eggs until hatching, which takes place after seven days; mature at 3–4 years; live up to seven years.

OTHER NAMES: Stone Catfish, Doogler, Whitecat, Deepwater Bullhead, Mongrel Bullhead, Stonecat Madtom, Beetle-eye.

DID YOU KNOW? The Stonecat is one of only three fishes in Canada with venomous spines.

STATUS: locally uncommon; undetermined status.

HABITAT: slow-moving water that contains large rocks and boulders, usually with gravel or silty bottoms.

ID: rounded body tapers to tail; **four pairs of barbels**—two pairs on lower jaw, one pair on sides of mouth and one pair near nares; long adipose fin; **anal fin is about same length as adipose fin;** obvious spines on pectoral and dorsal fins; **squared caudal fin** has light-coloured margin; brownish yellow above to whitish below.

SIMILAR SPECIES: *Burbot* (p. 134): one barbel on lower jaw; smaller and rounded caudal fin; skin has dark mottling; pelvic fins far forward on body, below or in front of pectorals; two dorsal fins, the first short and the second very long; anal fin as long as second dorsal fin.

Burbot

four pairs of barbels

long adipose fin equal in length to anal fin

squared caudal fin

LENGTH: *Average:* 15–20 cm. *Maximum:* 25 cm.

NORTHERN PIKE *Esox lucius*

STATUS: common; sensitive to overfishing.

HABITAT: vegetated edges of lakes and rivers; warm stretches of rivers with low to moderate current.

The Northern Pike's hunting style is to lie in wait in shallow water, camouflaged among aquatic vegetation, until an unsuspecting fish floats by. With a quick stab of its long snout, the Northern Pike ambushes the prey in its heavily toothed jaws. Fishes are not the only animals to fall prey to the Northern Pike's voracious appetite: ducklings, shorebirds and rodents are also sought after. • There is a myth among anglers that Northern Pike are not as easily caught in August because they lose their teeth. In fact, these fish do lose their teeth, but never all at the same time. Anglers find a decrease in the amount of biting pike in this month because of an increase in available prey and a warming of the water. By August, Northern Pike have usually moved to deeper, cooler waters. • The name "pike" comes from an Old English word for a primitive iron-tipped spear used in battle.

VIEWING TIPS: If you canoe slowly in the shallows in most Alberta lakes, you'll see adult Northern Pike hanging motionless amongst the reeds or along the edge of a dense aquatic plant bed. Young are seen closer to shore, right next to overhanging vegetation or undercut banks. They must stay in more shallow water to avoid the hungry jaws of their older aunts and uncles. • Pike spawning runs present an excellent opportunity to introduce someone to the joys of fishwatching. On one of the first nice, hot spring days, when most of the snow is gone, go for a drive around almost any big Alberta lake and find a bridge over a slow, marshy creek crossing. Some particularly good sites are Talbot Lake in Jasper National Park, Newell Lake near Brooks, Lac La Biche and Lac Ste. Anne. Watch patiently along grassy, brushy edges or at the base of beaver dams for spawning Northern Pike. They may rise out of the murky water to slowly swirl through the vegetation or quickly burst up and over the dam's spillway. Keep watching, and you may get the thrill of seeing a metre-long green beast cruising up the shallow water, pushing along a bow wave like a surface-running submarine.

FEEDING: carnivorous; ambushes prey by hiding within the aquatic vegetation; hunts during the day and mainly uses its sight; prefers Yellow Perch and other small fishes; also eats birds, rodents, amphibians and anything else that is available.

SPAWNING: early spring spawner; migrates to spawning grounds during the night or late evening; prefers heavily vegetated shallow bays and even flooded areas for spawning; one female is flanked by two or more males; female releases an average of 30,000 eggs over several days; 50–60 eggs are released during each spawning act; eggs stick to vegetation; eggs hatch after two weeks but remain attached to the vegetation for an extra week for protection; males mature in 3–5 years; females mature in 4–6 years; live up to 25 years.

OTHER NAMES: Jackfish, Shovelnose, Water Wolf.

DID YOU KNOW? In medieval culture legends abounded about the Northern Pike's size and age. Many hoaxes arose, including a pike mounted in Mannheim Cathedral in Germany that supposedly lived for 267 years.

ID: body is rounded in cross-section; **long, flat snout; terminal mouth; rounded dorsal fin is set far back, equal with rounded anal fin;** forked caudal fin; sharp, backward-slanted teeth, even on roof of mouth; "cheek" and upper half of operculum are scaly; dark green or brown with light yellowish spots. *Juvenile:* vertical stripes instead of spots.

SIMILAR SPECIES: none.

rounded dorsal fin parallel with anal fin

long snout with sharp teeth

LENGTH: *Average:* 40–50 cm. *Maximum:* 1.2 m.
WEIGHT: *Average:* 2–5 kg. *Maximum:* 17 kg.

CISCO   *Coregonus artedi*

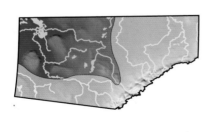

Early settlers named this species "Lake Herring" because of the massive numbers of individuals observed near shoals. Cisco spend their lives in large groups that are constantly on the move, usually in open water. They follow colder water to deeper layers in the summer. Where pollution nourishes algal blooms in lakes, the lack of oxygen in the water owing to decomposition of algae may lead to mass mortality. • Cisco are an important food source for predators such as Lake Trout, Northern Pike, Yellow Perch, Walleye and Burbot. During the occasional midsummer mass mortalities, Cisco form a key food item for fledgling ospreys and bald eagles. They are also the major host for the tapeworm *Triaenophorus crassus*, which is sometimes ingested when they eat small crustaceans. Although the tapeworm does not affect humans, all commercially caught whitefishes were once "candled" (held against a source of light) so that the cysts in the meat could be seen. Lake Whitefish are practically free of this parasite outside the range of Cisco south of the Athabasca River. Transfers of Walleye fry from northern Alberta to southern reservoirs for sport fishers unwittingly also introduced Cisco beyond their natural range, raising the unwelcome possibility of moving this economically disastrous parasite as well.

VIEWING TIPS: You'll seldom see a Cisco, but you can see signs of it. On calm summer evenings, watch the surface of our big northern lakes, including Lac La Biche (near the provincial park causeway is great), Lesser Slave Lake and Touchwood Lake. Rings as large as dinner plates mark where Cisco are enjoying meals of hatching midge larvae. Sometimes a school of fish will be so large that the rises will look and sound like a localized rain squall. It's an awesome experience to sit in a boat while one of these massive feeding schools passes around you. • In western and northern Canada, always tell your friends you saw a "Tullibee" (only biologists call them by the proper name Cisco).

FEEDING: feeds from the surface; eats mostly plankton; also eats fish eggs and fry, crustaceans and adult and larval invertebrates.

SPAWNING: late September to early December; usually in shallow water 1–3 m deep, over almost any kind of bottom but mostly gravel; males arrive in large schools on spawning grounds 2–5 days before females; eggs are slightly adhesive to the bottom; hatch in April or May; mature at about three years; usually live to 10 years but may live up to 30 years.

OTHER NAMES: Lake Herring, Tullibee, Blueback, Freshwater Herring, Grayback Tullibee, Common Cisco, Sand Herring, Bear Lake Herring.

STATUS: common; secure.

HABITAT: lakes and sometimes large rivers; prefers temperatures around 13° C; usually form large schools in mid-water, to 50 m deep, but may be found in shallower water.

DID YOU KNOW? Cisco are extremely variable in size, shape and colour among Alberta lakes and throughout the Canadian north. Some populations mature at the size of a minnow, while other populations grow to over 40 cm in length and weigh several kilograms before spawning. Sorting out the differences between the various forms, subspecies and species has kept scientists scratching their heads for over 100 years.

ID: slender; laterally compressed body; **large scales; small head and jaws;** terminal mouth; **gill rakers are long and numerous** (up to 48); base of adipose fin is narrow; bluish to olive dorsally; silvery on sides and belly.

SIMILAR SPECIES: *Shortjaw Cisco* (p. 106): usually fewer than 43 gill rakers. *Lake Whitefish* (p. 108): subterminal mouth.

Shortjaw Cisco

Lake Whitefish

small head and mouth

LENGTH: *Average:* 20–30 cm. *Maximum:* 45 cm.
WEIGHT: *Average:* 100–300 g. *Maximum:* 1 kg.

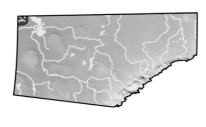

SHORTJAW CISCO *Coregonus zenithicus*

The Shortjaw Cisco is different from its close relative the Cisco in two main ways: the Shortjaw's lower jaw just slightly protrudes beyond the upper jaw and on average it has fewer gill rakers. • So far the only Alberta population of this species occurs in Barrow Lake, which is part of the Slave River drainage basin. While the number of fishes found in our province may be small, the Shortjaws found in Alberta seem to be larger in size than any other known populations. • Shortjaw Cisco were discovered in Duluth, Minnesota, at a fish-processing plant. Pressures from overfishing, competition from exotic species, lamprey predation and decreased water quality have taken a large toll on Shortjaw Cisco populations in the Great Lakes. Ichthyologists are still trying to figure out if the Shortjaw Cisco found in Alberta is related to those found in the Great Lakes area. Cisco species are so confusing that some fish biologists are now lumping them into one large Cisco complex.

VIEWING TIPS: There are not many viewing opportunities in Alberta for Shortjaw Cisco. Barrow Lake is the best place to look, and possibly Lake Athabasca. Fly-in anglers vacationing at the myriad of lakes north of Fort Chipewyan should keep a close eye on little whitefishes that they find in trout or pike tummies. Careful examination of the big fishes' dinners may reveal a new population of Shortjaw Cisco, and the keen-eyed, lucky angler will get his or her name mentioned in the scientific literature. •

FEEDING: filter-feeder; eats plankton and crustaceans, especially opossum shrimp.

SPAWNING: November to December; usually spawns over clay but will use many different substrates; males arrive on spawning grounds 2–5 days before females; eggs sink and are slightly adhesive to the bottom; eggs hatch in April or May; mature at about three years; live up to 10 years.

OTHER NAMES: Light-back Tullibee, Shortjaw Chub, Longjaw.

DID YOU KNOW? The species name *zenithicus* comes from the nickname for the city in which the Shortjaw Cisco was discovered. Duluth, Minnesota, was dubbed the "Zenith City" in a railway advertisement in the late 1800s.

STATUS: rare; may be at risk.

HABITAT: prefers shallow lake waters in Alberta but frequents deep water in the East.

ID: white to silvery body; dark blue or green dorsally; **large scales; small head and jaws;** terminal mouth; relatively vertical tip of snout; lower jaw sometimes protrudes beyond upper jaw; upper jaw relatively long; **relatively few and short gill rakers** (usually fewer than 43); bluish to olive dorsally; silvery on sides and belly.

SIMILAR SPECIES: *Cisco* (p. 104): gill rakers are more numerous and longer.

Cisco

small head and mouth

LENGTH: *Average:* 27–40 cm. *Maximum:* 51 cm.

LAKE WHITEFISH   *Coregonus clupeaformis*

Although the Lake Whitefish lives in the depths of lakes, you are more likely to encounter this species than other whitefishes. On a calm evening, you may see the dorsal fin cut through the surface as the fish rises gently and swallows a floating insect. Its well-known shape is formed by a small head that flows through a hump on the back into a broad, silvery body. The hump is not a reliable field mark, because its size depends on the age of the fish. • Lake Whitefish live in most of the larger lakes in Alberta. They were also introduced beyond their natural range into irrigation reservoirs in southern Alberta because of their popularity with commercial fishers. In Lake Wabamun, west of Edmonton, up to 270,000 kg of Lake Whitefish are taken by the commercial fishery each year. They are also the main catch in the popular activity of ice fishing on Alberta's lakes, and spawning runs at shallow lakeshores are an exceptional sight for fishwatchers. • A huge Lake Whitefish that weighed 19 kg was caught in Lake Superior in 1918.

VIEWING TIPS: Although it sounds kind of romantic for a fish book, imagine a moonlit autumn night, with a canoe drifting slowly over the gravel beach of a calm, placid lake. Now picture a thousand frenzied Lake Whitefish dashing about in the shallows under the canoe. Looking for spawning Lake Whitefish is an excellent excuse to go for a nighttime canoe jaunt. If you're in the right place at the right time, the water around and below you will be filled with dark forms racing past in blissful ignorance of

any terrestrial interlopers. Some will thump right into the side of your canoe in their passion-blinded state (and that is one startling noise in the dark of the night!). One of the most accessible spots for fishwatching in October and November is northeastern Wabamun Lake at the railway trestle where Halfmoon Bay joins the main lake. Other good fishwatching sites include Lac Ste. Anne (offshore from Castle Island) and Talbot Lake in Jasper National Park, which is best when the ice is strong enough to walk on but still clear enough to see through.

FEEDING: benthic feeder; feeds on larval insects (particularly *Chironomidae* midges), snails, clams, fish eggs and sometimes small fishes; sometimes pelagic; sifts for plankton; occasionally takes insects from the surface.

SPAWNING: late September to early winter when water temperatures fall below 8° C; spawning lasts 2–6 weeks; usually in water 2–4 m deep on gravelly or sandy shoals of large lakes; migrates into tributaries occasionally; no nest; eggs hatch in April and May; mature at 7–8 years; live to 15 years.

OTHER NAMES: Humpback Whitefish, Common Whitefish, Eastern Whitefish, Great Lakes Whitefish, Inland Whitefish, Labrador Whitefish, Tittimeg (Cree).

DID YOU KNOW? The word "angler" comes from the Sanskrit word "anka," referring to the angle of the hook.

STATUS: common; secure.

HABITAT: cool, deep water at the bottom of large lakes; prefers water temperatures of 10–13° C; usually at depths of about 10 m, sometimes as deep as 100 m; occasionally in rivers.

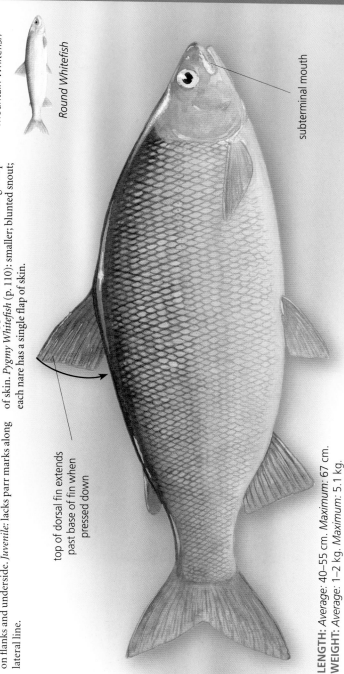

Mountain Whitefish

Round Whitefish

subterminal mouth

top of dorsal fin extends
past base of fin when
pressed down

ID: laterally compressed body; **subterminal mouth; top of dorsal fin extends past base of fin when pressed down;** small head; two flaps of skin between nares; larger fish develop characteristic hump behind head; forked caudal fin; bluish dorsally, changing to white and silver on flanks and underside. *Juvenile:* lacks parr marks along lateral line.

SIMILAR SPECIES: *Mountain Whitefish* (p. 114): develops an upturned snout when spawning; has a more pointed snout; each nare has a single flap of skin. *Round Whitefish* (p. 112): body is rounded in cross-section; brown spots on upper sides; each nare has a single flap of skin. *Pygmy Whitefish* (p. 110): smaller; blunted snout; each nare has a single flap of skin.

LENGTH: *Average:* 40–55 cm. *Maximum:* 67 cm.
WEIGHT: *Average:* 1–2 kg. *Maximum:* 5.1 kg.

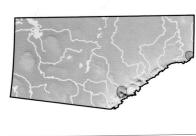

PYGMY WHITEFISH *Prosopium coulteri*

We know very little about this small and inconspicuous fish, which lives deep in lakes and mountain streams. The species was first described from the Kickinghorse River at Field, British Columbia, in 1892, by fish biologist Carl H. Eigenmann during a sampling expedition along the Canadian Pacific Railway. It was found again throughout the Rockies and in Alaska, but it was not until 1952 that the Pygmy Whitefish was discovered in eastern Canada in Lake Superior, living in waters more than 55 m deep. • During the ice age most of Alberta was covered with ice, and fishes survived in streams to the south. When the ice melted and retreated, large, cold lakes formed nearby, offering ideal conditions for Pygmy Whitefish. As the climate warmed further, this species remained only in the mountains and at the cold bottoms of larger lakes. • Pygmy Whitefish are difficult to tell apart from young Mountain Whitefish and have probably been misidentified in many places in the Rockies.

VIEWING TIPS: Solomon Creek and the mouth of the Snake Indian River (both between Hinton and Jasper along the Athabasca River) and Waterton Lakes are the only known Alberta locations for this animal. Keep a sharp lookout in foothill streams in those areas. If you do see a Pygmy Whitefish (especially in the northern foothills), you'll be immortalized by the Alberta fish-lover community. Anglers catching Mountain

Whitefish should pay close attention to small whitefish with chunky heads and big eyes. Take a photo or draw a sketch and tell your local biologist. • As with the Mountain Whitefish, your best bet for viewing is during the spawning run, when these fish might appear in shallow riffles in the low, clear autumn flows. Stream snorkellers have had some success spotting these unique fish in the clear waters of northern British Columbia.

FEEDING: mostly benthic; feeds on larval invertebrates, crustaceans, small molluscs and the eggs of trouts and whitefishes.

SPAWNING: October to December; probably in shallow water in lakes or streams; females release about 500 eggs per spawning season; no nest; eggs are shed over gravel and incubate until spring; mature at 1–3 years; live to eight years.

OTHER NAMES: Coulter's Whitefish, Brownback Whitefish.

DID YOU KNOW? The Pygmy Whitefish was first discovered in Alberta in 1966 in Solomon Creek, but these museum specimens were misidentified until 1984. The first properly identified specimens were found in 1971, when two individuals were netted at a depth of 50 m in Upper Waterton Lake.

STATUS: rare; may be at risk.

HABITAT: mountainous lakes and streams that can be silty or clear; in lakes, usually deeper than 6 m.

ID: body rounded in cross-section and elongated; small head; **rounded snout with slightly subterminal mouth; top of dorsal fin does not extend past base of fin when pressed down;** small adipose fin; dark brown dorsally; silvery on sides; whitish below. *Spawning male:* nuptial tubercles on head and paired fins. *Juvenile:* several parr marks along lateral line.

SIMILAR SPECIES: *Mountain Whitefish* (p. 114): larger adipose fin; bulbous snout; smaller scales. *Round Whitefish* (p. 112): larger; body rounded in cross-section; brown spots on upper sides; snout pointed. *Lake Whitefish* (p. 108): much larger; more laterally compressed; double nasal flap.

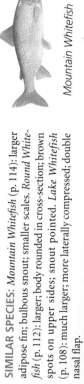

Mountain Whitefish

Round Whitefish

top of dorsal fin doesn't extend past base of fin when pressed down

spawning

LENGTH: *Average:* 10 cm. *Maximum:* 13 cm.

ROUND WHITEFISH
Prosopium cylindraceum

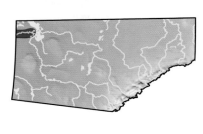

The Round Whitefish is the more cylindrical northern counterpart of the Mountain Whitefish. The southern parts of the Round Whitefish's range reach into Alberta's Peace–Athabasca Delta. This species is found more often in lakes in the southern regions of its range but will inhabit streams and tundra ponds in the Far North. • During the last ice age, the Round Whitefish was probably split from the Mountain Whitefish into separated refugia. Afterward, the Round Whitefish spread into our area from Alaska and the Yukon, and the Mountain Whitefish dispersed northward from the Columbia River and Missouri River systems. • The Round Whitefish is one of the most colourful whitefishes in Alberta—the males show off orange-tinted pectoral fins during spawning. Males migrate to the spawning grounds earlier than females, and courtship takes place in pairs. Eggs are released mostly over gravel, but Round Whitefish also spawn over aquatic vegetation and silty bottoms.

VIEWING TIPS: There have been only three sightings of this fish in Alberta, all of them from Wood Buffalo National Park and its vicinity. Any small, cigar-shaped whitefish seen downstream of Fort McMurray should be looked at with great interest and care. • If you are interested in going a bit farther afield, viewing is great north of the Alberta border. Round Whitefish in tundra ponds can behave just like Alberta's more common Mountain Whitefish, splashing around and joyously packing their little bellies with the incredibly bountiful bug life of arctic summers.

FEEDING: benthic feeder; feeds on larval invertebrates, small clams and snails, eggs of Lake Trout and other species and small fishes, such as sculpins and sticklebacks.

SPAWNING: October to December; no nest or parental care; over gravel or vegetation in lakes from 3–15 m deep or at the mouth of streams; occasionally in rivers; eggs hatch in April; mature at 5–7 years; live up to 14 years.

OTHER NAMES: Round Fish, Frost Fish, Pilot Fish, Grayback, Menominee, Cross Whitefish, Lake Minnow.

DID YOU KNOW? In New England, Round Whitefish are sometimes called "Shad Waiters" because they are known to wait around where shad are spawning and then eat their eggs. Round Whitefish exhibit the same behaviour on the northern spawning grounds of Longnose Suckers.

STATUS: rare; undetermined status.

HABITAT: shallow parts of large lakes, usually above 40 m in depth; large rivers and streams.

Mountain Whitefish

Pygmy Whitefish

ID: slender, **cylindrical body,** nearly round at midsection; small head; snout looks round when viewed from side and looks "pinched" or laterally compressed in frontal view; **top of dorsal fin does not extend past base of fin when pressed down;** amber colour to lower fins; brown spots on adipose fin and sometimes on head; back is bronze to greenish grey; silvery sides and belly. *Spawning:* orange-tinted pectoral fins.

SIMILAR SPECIES: *Mountain Whitefish* (p. 114): body more laterally compressed; bulbous snout; larger adipose fin. *Pygmy Whitefish* (p. 110): smaller; blunted snout. *Lake Whitefish* (p. 108): laterally compressed; caudal fin deeply forked; rounded snout.

top of dorsal fin doesn't extend past base of fin when pressed down

spawning

LENGTH: *Average:* 20–30 cm. *Maximum:* 35 cm.
WEIGHT: *Average:* 100–200 g. *Maximum:* 300 g.

MOUNTAIN WHITEFISH · *Prosopium williamsoni*

Mountain Whitefish of Alberta's Eastern Slopes have endured habitat changes and increased fishing pressures remarkably well. Known affectionately as "Rockies," they are common in every major river system in the foothills, and they range along the Athabasca River and Peace River drainage basins far into the northeastern part of the province. • Some Mountain Whitefish can be sedentary, but this species is known for its migratory behaviour (one tagged Rocky went from the mouth of La Biche River all the way up the Athabasca River into Jasper National Park—a distance of over 500 km!). Large numbers of whitefish school upstream in rivers such as the Red Deer in autumn, en route to their spawning grounds. In fact, Mountain Whitefish seem in constant migration between seasonal feeding habitat, and they move in schools from pool to pool. Juveniles travel together in shallow water at shorelines or in protected backwaters. They do not seek cover in rocks as trouts typically do, relying on safety in numbers.

VIEWING TIPS: In summer, watch for splashes on the water's surface in big river pools. At dusk, insects fill the warm air, and Rockies switch from bottom-feeders to leaping bug-eaters. • Autumn spawning runs give fish-lovers good opportunities to see big bunches of Rockies in clear, shallow water. Riffles on big rivers (such as the McLeod, Snaring and Bow rivers) or gravelly stretches in tiny foothill streams will have schools of Mountain Whitefish massed for the big event. Deep pools at the end of a shallow riffle section are prime spawning sites—watch at the shallow tail-out of the pool. If you can creep close to an overhanging bank, peer down and you can sometimes spot individuals at close range, hugging the calm water in stream-edge pools. Irrigation canals in southern Alberta are also good places to look for these fish in autumn, when water is low. At this time, many whitefish get stranded, and fish-lovers congregate to move them out to the deeper river areas in the Annual Great Alberta Fish Rescue. Contact Trout Unlimited in Calgary for details. • In winter, look for them below the Dickson Dam on the Red Deer River.

FEEDING: feeds mostly on benthic invertebrates, including aquatic insect larvae and molluscs; sometimes takes fish eggs, smaller fishes and terrestrial insects from the surface.

SPAWNING: late September to November; migrates to spawning grounds in the main stem of fast rivers or in tributaries, sometimes gravelly lakeshores; courtship begins in the evening; spawning takes place at night over gravelly area; no nest or parental care; eggs hatch from March to April when the ice breaks; young form schools; mature in 3–4 years; usually live up to 18 years, but the oldest Alberta Rocky known was 29 years old.

OTHER NAMES: Williamson's Whitefish, Rocky Mountain Whitefish.

STATUS: locally abundant; secure.

HABITAT: inhabits rivers and fast, clear or silty areas of larger streams; also in cold, deep lakes but rarely below 20 m; can be either resident or migratory; in streams, it moves from riffles in summer to large pools in winter.

bulbous snout

Lake Whitefish

Round Whitefish

top of dorsal fin doesn't extend past base of fin when pressed down

DID YOU KNOW? Mountain Whitefish that inhabit rivers may have thinner bodies and slightly upturned, bulbous snouts that help them to flip over stones in search of invertebrates. These individuals are sometimes called "Pinocchios" or "Bugle-noses."

ID: slender, cylindrical body; small head; **bulbous snout; subterminal mouth**; large, coarse scales; forked caudal fin; **top of dorsal fin does not extend past base of fin when pressed down**; dark brown or blue dorsally; silvery sides. *Juvenile:* young have 7–11 large oval parr marks (sometimes with a few spots above).

SIMILAR SPECIES: *Lake Whitefish* (p. 108): two nare flaps; somewhat subterminal mouth. *Round Whitefish* (p. 112): body is rounded in cross-section; brown spots on upper sides; snout is pointed; known only from the Lake Athabasca area. *Pygmy Whitefish* (p. 110): smaller; blunt snout; larger scales.

LENGTH: *Average:* 25–45 cm. *Maximum:* 63 cm.
WEIGHT: *Average:* 0.5–1.3 kg. *Maximum:* 2.6 kg.

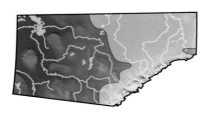

ARCTIC GRAYLING *Thymallus arcticus*

Brilliant coloration and an enlarged dorsal fin play a large part in the biology of the Arctic Grayling, and this member of the trout family is often praised as one of Alberta's most beautiful fishes. Spawning males are more intensely coloured than females, showing off their virility as they migrate from lakes and large rivers to small tributaries. At the spawning site, each male aggressively defends a private area tucked in between some rocks. Any male intruder is challenged first with a threat display that shows off the raised dorsal fin and gaping mouth. If this move proves ineffective, the intruder is attacked directly and chased off the territory. Females enter the territory by adopting a submissive pose, with their dorsal fin depressed and tail and body resting on the stream bed. • A fish of cold and clear streams, the Arctic Grayling is vulnerable to changes in the environment. It needs to see its food to catch it, so clean, clear water is important. It is at the southern edge of its range in Alberta, and climate change may result in water that is too warm for this arctic species. • Although the Arctic Grayling eats mostly aquatic insects, it will occasionally swallow voles that get too close to the water's edge!

VIEWING TIPS: This fish is fun to watch if you're near a northern stream on a summer evening. Some good places to try are Sundance Creek along Highway 16 west of Edson, the McLeod River upstream of Edson, the Pembina River at

the Highway 40 crossing and the Little Smoky River. Wear a bug shirt and stand near a strip of fast water below a pool. (Unlike members of the trout subfamily, these fish seem to prefer the faster water more than the pools, although they are found in both.) Watch for bugs drifting down or unlucky stoneflies skimming the surface while laying eggs. If Arctic Grayling are present, there will be a flurry of leaps and splashes as they compete for dinner. Grayling are spectacular aerialists and will occasionally collide in mid-air when going for the same choice morsel.

FEEDING: opportunistic; picks terrestrial insects, such as beetles, ants, wasps and grasshoppers, from the water's surface (often more than half of diet); also eats aquatic insects, small fishes and eggs, crustaceans, molluscs and occasionally shrews and voles.

SPAWNING: May to June; spawns in 5–10° C water; migrates to small, gravelly streams just after ice break-up; spawns during the day, mostly in the afternoon; no nest; eggs hatch after 13–18 days; young stay in the same stream until freeze-up; mature at four years; live to eight years.

OTHER NAMES: Grayling, American Grayling, Bluefish, Back's Grayling, Sailfin Arctic Grayling, Arctic Trout.

STATUS: common; sensitive.

HABITAT: clear, cold waters of large rivers, gravelly creeks and lakes; usually near the surface in lakes; is sometimes found in glacial waters.

DID YOU KNOW? The Latin name *thymallus* refers to the supposed odour of thyme in the fresh fish, but few, if any, biologists working with grayling have ever smelled that odour coming from this elegant fish. It looks very beautiful but smells very bad.

ID: elongated and laterally compressed body; **long, large dorsal fin; black spots on anterior part of body;** silver body; dorsal fin has rows of orange spots and a few emerald green spots and is edged with red or orange; large eyes; forked caudal fin. *Male:* dorsal fin is very large.

SIMILAR SPECIES: none.

long, large dorsal fin

black spots near front of body

LENGTH: *Average:* 30–40 cm. *Maximum:* 55 cm.
WEIGHT: *Average:* 300–800 g. *Maximum:* 1.3 kg.

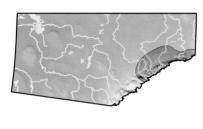

HABITAT: mountain streams and tributaries; alpine lakes; clean, clear, oxygen-rich water; can be found at colder temperatures than Rainbow Trout.

CUTTHROAT TROUT

Oncorhynchus clarki

Although sometimes misleading, one of the main characteristics used to distinguish this species from other black-spotted trouts is the two orange to red lines in the gular folds on each side of a Cutthroat's lower jaw. It is misleading because young cutthroats may not have these slashes, and if the fish dies they can disappear in a matter of hours. Alberta's native Athabasca Rainbow Trout, which sports a pale orange throat slash, will also fool you, as will hybrids between Cutthroats and Rainbows. The only way to really tell if you have a Cutthroat is to put your fingers in its mouth (recommended for dead fish only!) and feel for the raspy teeth at the base of the tongue. • Fourteen subspecies of Cutthroats have been described so far. The *lewisi* subspecies was named "Westslope Cutthroat" but it is also native to the Eastern Slopes of the Rockies in Alberta and Montana. • Once abundant in Banff National Park and the Bow River and South Saskatchewan River systems, native Cutthroat populations declined throughout the early 20th century. These fish were subsequently restocked and were also introduced to other streams along Alberta's Eastern Slopes, but the released fish were the Yellowstone subspecies of Cutthroat Trout, Rainbow Trout and hybrids of the two. As a result, Westslope Cutthroats and native Rainbow Trout were often displaced by the introduced fish. Pure native populations of Westslope Cutthroat are only known from the Picklejar Lakes and perhaps a small number of mountain lakes in Banff National Park.

VIEWING TIPS: Late summer, a swarm of grasshoppers and low, clear water are ideal conditions for watching Cutthroat Trout in Alberta. The best places to look for them are the upper Ram River, near the Forestry Trunk Road, streams in the Porcupine Hills and the upper Oldman River. Tiny mountain or foothill tributary streams will be home to packs of juvenile Cutts. Sneak carefully up small pools or calm stretches of deeper water and watch for the little minnowlike trouts darting about as minuscule insects come drifting into their feeding range. To see larger Cutts takes more patience. Pull up a stump alongside a large river where you can see good hiding places along the river bottom (boulders, broken slabs of rock or submerged logs and brush). Be still, watch and wait. In good spots, you will almost always be rewarded by seeing a fish glide out of the shadows, gulp a drifting bug and slide back into cover. Once you spot the fish, keep watching. You'll start to see how it carefully judges the distance to the bugs and balances getting food with the risk of becoming food.

FEEDING: eats aquatic and terrestrial invertebrates, crustaceans, frogs, small fishes and their eggs (mostly trouts, sculpins and sticklebacks).

SPAWNING: early May to mid-June, when water reaches 10° C; in gravelly tributaries; female digs a redd; she lies in the nest for fertilization; female dislodges gravel upstream of the nest to cover eggs; eggs hatch after 6–7 weeks; mature at 2–4 years; live to eight years.

OTHER NAMES: Westslope Cutthroat, Native Trout, Redthroated Trout, Short-tailed Trout, Yellowstone Cutthroat, Harvest Trout, Black-spotted Trout.

DID YOU KNOW? The novella *A River Runs Through It* by Norman MacLean involves native Cutthroat Trout in Montana. When the movie based on the novella was made, filmmakers needed to use hatchery-raised Rainbow Trout because of the low numbers and small size of the remaining Cutthroat Trout.

ID: variable in colour owing to hybridization and subspecies; **light body with black spots** that are usually concentrated above lateral line and near back part of body and fins in Westslope species; **bright red streaks in gular folds of lower jaw;** pinkish "cheeks"; pink extends down lateral line. *Juvenile:* 10 parr marks along lateral line.

SIMILAR SPECIES: *Rainbow Trout* (p. 120): no minute teeth at base of tongue; absence of gular slash is an unreliable field mark.

Rainbow Trout

Westslope Cutthroat

red slash on throat

LENGTH: *Average:* 20–40 cm. *Maximum:* 74 cm.
WEIGHT: *Average:* 200–500 g. *Maximum:* 4.3 kg.

RAINBOW TROUT *Oncorhynchus mykiss*

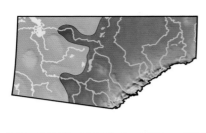

Because of anglers' love for this fish, the Rainbow Trout has spread from western North America to every continent except Antarctica. It is distinguished by a colourful appearance with heavy black spotting on its back and sides; otherwise, variation is the rule. • Alberta's only native Rainbow Trout are found in the Athabasca River drainage basin and belong to one of the slowest-growing and smallest strains in the world. They are found from the headwaters to the southern reaches of Swan Hills. • Rainbow Trout are highly respected by fly fishers because of their impressive jumps and their fighting strength. Rainbow Trout have been introduced throughout the globe, and beginning in the 1930s many of Alberta's rivers were stocked with fish of different origin and genetic composition than our native fish. The introduced fish hybridized with local fish and displaced other native species of the trout family. • Rainbow Trout are the popular choice for "put and take" fishing. Pothole lakes surrounding urban areas are stocked with these fish to ease the angling pressure on local, native stocks and provide local recreation for anglers. • A whopping monster of a Rainbow Trout was found in British Columbia—it weighed 24 kg.

VIEWING TIPS: Rainbow Trout are stocked in farmer's dugouts and small-town fish ponds all over Alberta, but many people prefer to look for them where they are native: in montane habitat. The Maligne River in Jasper National Park, where it leaves Maligne Lake, is a great spot to see huge lake Rainbows spawning in June, and some fish even stick around in this open water for winter viewing. Foothill streams in the Coalbranch area (south of Hinton) are other good places to look. If you go in August, the stream flows are low and clear and the streamside meadows are full of grasshoppers. Sneak up to the bank and toss a small hopper well upstream. Watch the water just under the insect, because the real treat is seeing the little Rainbow rise up from the dark depths and contemplate its dinner before slurping it down. You can spend whole afternoons playing with and admiring this gorgeous Alberta native in the tiny trickles of foothill streams that it loves.

FEEDING: eats aquatic insects, mostly small shrimp; also eats snails, leeches, other fishes and eggs if available.

SPAWNING: April to late June; introduced stocks spawn earlier than native populations; high elevation delays spawning; spawning occurs in running water, such as at small tributaries of rivers or inlets of lakes; usually over fine gravel; female digs a large redd with her caudal fin; she is flanked by one or two males and releases her eggs; she uses her tail to loosen gravel upstream to cover the eggs, which hatch in late July to September; mature in 3–4 years; live up to 13 years.

OTHER NAMES: Steelhead, Kamloops Trout, Pacific Trout, Silver Trout, Redband Trout, Redband, Gerrard Trout, Half-pounder.

STATUS: *Introduced populations:* common; secure. *Native populations:* locally common; threatened.

HABITAT: cool, oxygen-rich waters; open, meadow streams; prefers stretches of swift-flowing water, edges of strong currents, heads of rapids or strong riffles; has been introduced to shallow "pothole" lakes.

Cutthroat Trout

Golden Trout

pinkish "cheek" and body

DID YOU KNOW? *Mykiss* is actually pronounced "mee-kiss." It is the name for this fish in Kamchatka, a north-eastern Russian language.

ID: bluish to olive back; silver, yellowish green or pinkish sides with **black spots over whole body including fins**; rounded head; **pink blush on "cheeks"**; some individuals have orange gular slash; rectangular dorsal fin; squarish caudal fin. *Spawning:* red line along body. *Juvenile:* 8–12 parr marks; these marks may remain on adults at higher elevations.

SIMILAR SPECIES: *Cutthroat Trout* (p. 118): has basi-branchial teeth inside of mouth, near back of tongue. *Golden Trout* (p. 122): smaller; more golden colour; dark spots are concentrated near tail; only in a few lakes north of Waterton National Park.

LENGTH: *Average:* 30–45 cm. *Maximum:* 81 cm.
WEIGHT: *Average:* 0.5–1.5 kg. *Maximum:* 9.2 kg.

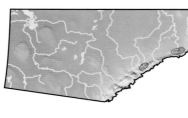

GOLDEN TROUT
Oncorhynchus mykiss aguabonita

The Golden Trout is a unique subspecies of Rainbow Trout that has been beautifying a few of Alberta's mountain lakes since its introduction in 1959. It was brought to Alberta for anglers wishing for a more challenging and picturesque location to fish in. • The Golden Trout is a rare and highly prized fish, and because of its slow growth, many rules and regulations are associated with it; for example, only one fish is allowed per angler. • Golden Trout are native to the high, cold lakes and streams of the Sierra Nevada in California. They are so strikingly beautiful that California made them their state fish. In our province, they are found in the Castle River system north of Waterton Lakes National Park and are stocked in a few other lakes in the Nordegg area. Alberta is the only province in Canada in which these gorgeous fish live.

VIEWING TIPS: Be prepared for a good hike if you want to observe these alpine jewels. The lakes they inhabit are always quite a distance from the nearest parking lot, but these fish are well worth the climb. South Fork (also known as Barnaby Lakes) and Rainy Ridge lakes southwest of Pincher Creek have the easiest access, but you will still have to hike for a while. The Golden Trout's stunning colour pattern and the crystal-clear mountain water make for excellent viewing. Watch along the shore of alpine lakes or slip quietly alongside the outflow streams, looking first for the shadow of a fish in the bright summer sunshine, then spotting the slowly undulating form of a Golden as it hovers in the current or cruises for summer bugs. Careful use of a fly rod will probably give you the best view of this Californian's amazing colours.

FEEDING: eats aquatic insects (adults and larvae) and zooplankton.

SPAWNING: late June to early July; female digs out more than one redd in gravelly areas in the mouths of rivers; she releases about 2000 eggs per redd; more than one male fertilizes the eggs, which may hatch as late as September; mature at 3–4 years; live up to seven years.

OTHER NAMES: California Golden Trout.

DID YOU KNOW? *Aguabonita* means "beautiful water" in Spanish, a fitting species name for this colourful fish.

STATUS: rare; introduced.

HABITAT: cold, oxygen-rich, high-elevation lakes; found in high-elevation streams in its native area of California; along gravelly and rocky shores.

Rainbow Trout

Cutthroat Trout

parr marks

spots concentrated
near tail

ID: small, golden body with red along lateral line and belly; **vertical parr marks** may be present along lateral line, up to 10 lines per side; black spots along back and dorsal fin, **spots concentrated on caudal peduncle and squared caudal fin;** white tips on lower fins.

SIMILAR SPECIES: *Rainbow Trout* (p. 120): black spots over entire body; pinkish "cheeks"; larger scales. *Cutthroat Trout* (p. 118): basibranchial teeth; red slash along gular fold (throat); spots over most of body, especially above lateral line.

LENGTH: *Average:* 15–25 cm. *Maximum:* 50 cm.
WEIGHT: *Average:* 300–400 g. *Maximum:* 2 kg.

BROWN TROUT

Salmo trutta

This classical trout has been so much a part of European heritage that early settlers brought it with them to different regions of the world, introducing the Brown Trout not only to Canada, but also to the United States, Chile, Argentina, South Africa, Australia and New Zealand. Today, some of the largest populations of Brown Trout in western Canada are found in the rivers of central Alberta. The Brown Trout population in the Bow River system through Banff and Calgary in particular is known for its abundance and large sizes. • The Brown Trout is a drift feeder and is similar to the introduced Brook Trout in its preference for streams with cover and a moderate flow of water. It can handle warmer water temperatures and higher turbidity than native members of the trout family, and as a result it has been introduced to streams that have been disturbed by logging or industrial activity. It is a competitive fish, and it has contributed to the decline of native trout species in Alberta. • The Brown Trout is a true trout species, but its closest relative is the Atlantic Salmon. On both eastern and western coasts of Canada and in other parts of the world, the Brown Trout can be anadromous, inhabiting the ocean as an adult and returning to streams only for spawning.

VIEWING TIPS: In late October and November (when most tourists are gone and the hotels are cheap), go to Bill Griffiths Creek on the Bow River near Canmore. A parking area and fish-viewing site have been set up near some

of the best Brown Trout spawning flats on the entire Bow River. By simply standing along the shore, you can watch females dig redds and the great chase scenes that develop as infidelity is attempted and the perpetrators punished. Dress warm, pack a lunch and make a day of it. • The Bow River in Calgary and Raven Creek south of Rocky Mountain House are also good places to look for Brown Trout.

FEEDING: opportunistic drift feeder; usually nocturnal; hides under cover and bolts out to catch prey; eats invertebrates, shrimp, molluscs, fishes and frogs.

SPAWNING: October to December, when water temperatures fall below 8–10° C; in shallow, gravel beds of streams or at outlets of lakes; female digs a redd and covers eggs with gravel after fertilization; young hatch from March to late April; mature at 2–3 years, live up to 13 years.

OTHER NAMES: German Brown Trout, English Brown Trout, European Brown Trout, German Trout, English Trout, von Behr Trout, Lochleven Trout, Spotted Trout, Brownie.

DID YOU KNOW? The Brown Trout was first purposefully introduced to Alberta in 1924 by the provincial government to Raven River and Jasper National Park. In 1925, a hatchery truck broke down just upstream of Canmore near the Carrot Creek Bridge. Rather than let the fry die,

STATUS: common; introduced.

HABITAT: streams; deep pools under cover such as overhanging vegetation, undercut banks; larger rivers, beaver ponds and lakes; tolerant to turbidity and temperatures up to 24° C.

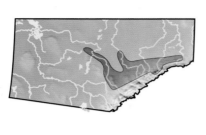

the operator released them into the creek, and the trout reached the Bow River system. The fish were likely from the variety that originated in Loch Leven, Scotland.

ID: golden brown or olive back and flanks; whitish underside; body, dorsal fin and adipose fin covered with dark spots, **some red spots with bluish halos;** some dark spots are large and irregularly shaped; caudal fin may have spots, especially along margins. *Juvenile:* forked caudal fin.

SIMILAR SPECIES: *Bull Trout* (p. 126): pinkish spots on body are lighter than olive background colour; white leading edges on bottom fins; upper jaw is longer and downturned. *Rainbow Trout* (p. 120) and *Cutthroat Trout* (p. 118): dark spots smaller and more plentiful; no red spots with blue halos; pinkish hue, especially near "cheek"; possibly a red gular slash on throat.

Bull Trout

Rainbow Trout

red spots with bluish halos on a light body

squared caudal fin may have spots

LENGTH: *Average:* 25–40 cm. *Maximum:* 87 cm.
WEIGHT: *Average:* 0.5–1 kg. *Maximum:* 7.9 kg.

BULL TROUT
Salvelinus confluentus

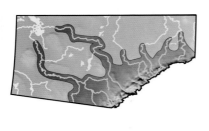

As Alberta's provincial fish, the Bull Trout has become a symbol for healthy river systems. This beautiful trout was once common in all streams with headwaters in the Eastern Slopes of the Rocky Mountains. In fact, at the turn of the century, the population stretched beyond the cities of Edmonton, Calgary and Lethbridge. Since then, Bull Trout have declined in numbers and distribution. Their habit of spawning in small and shallow creeks makes them vulnerable to bears, osprey and particularly people. Overfishing has been a major factor in this species' decline in Alberta because it is unusually easy to catch. Other factors that have affected its decline include loss of habitat, blocked migration routes (caused by dams and road crossings of streams), and changes in water quality caused by industrial activity and soil erosion. Competition and interbreeding by the introduced Brook Trout may have contributed further to the decline. Today, all remaining populations in the province are protected from harvest by anglers. "No black, put it back!" is an easy saying that refers to the lack of black spots on the Bull Trout's dorsal fin and helps anglers to identify this fish.

VIEWING TIPS: Bull Trout are often the only fishes in the fastest, steepest sections of mountain streams. These spectacular fish are best seen in September and early October, when the big adults have moved upstream into small tributary streams to spawn. The best sites for watching Bull Trout are Smith-Dorrien Creek, which flows into Lower Kananaskis Lake, Highwood River and tributaries of the upper McLeod River. Look along big, gravelly flats, ideally near logjams or overhanging brush. The big fish are well camouflaged with their silt grey backs, so watch carefully (polarized sunglasses are a must). Stay hidden in the shoreline brush and watch for the females to roll over on their sides to dig the redd. Males will rush around, showing off their testosterone-enlarged jaws and generally acting like teenage boys at a high-school dance. Juvenile Bull Trout will also be found in these areas year-round, but they are usually nocturnal and are seldom seen by bank-side gazers. Extreme-sport fishwatchers have had good luck viewing these young Bulls by snorkelling and swim-crawling along the freezing streams at night, shining underwater lights.

FEEDING: preys on other fishes, especially Mountain Whitefish; also feeds on aquatic invertebrates, crustaceans, and molluscs; will take insects floating on the water's surface.

SPAWNING: September to early October, in water with a temperature below 10° C; migrates to small, shallow creeks in August; female digs a large redd in gravel and covers the eggs after spawning; eggs hatch in March or April and stay in creeks for 1–3 years; mature at 3–6 years; adults often spawn every two years; may live to 20 years.

OTHER NAMES: Mountain Char, Western Brook Trout, Inland Char.

STATUS: uncommon; sensitive.

HABITAT: clear, cold streams and lakes; in larger rivers, more often in pools than in fast-moving water; in lakes at various depths; as adults, they are in gravelly streams with low sediment loads; young fish inhabit small, clear and shallow creeks fed by groundwater springs that are high in oxygen.

DID YOU KNOW? Until 1978, Bull Trout and coastal Dolly Varden were considered to belong to the same species. Then it became clear that no interbreeding takes place between our stream-loving Bull Trout and its sea-loving cousin. The Bull Trout's upper jaw is more downturned than that of the Dolly Varden, making this trout look mean and "bullish."

ID: olive green to tan body; whitish yellow, pink or red spots on back and sides; **no black marks on dorsal fin;** lower fins have white leading edge; **upper jaw is long and downturned; head is cone-shaped.** *Spawning male:* orange to red belly.

SIMILAR SPECIES: *Brown Trout* (p. 124): black markings on dorsal fin; light body with large, irregular dark spots and red spots with blue haloes. *Brook Trout* (p. 128): light spots on dark body, including red spots with blue haloes; dark spots on dorsal fin.

Brown Trout

Brook Trout

cone-shaped head

downturned and long upper jaw

no markings on dorsal fin

LENGTH: *Average:* 40–50 cm. *Maximum:* 85 cm.
WEIGHT: *Average:* 1–2 kg. *Maximum:* 8.1 kg.

BROOK TROUT

Salvelinus fontinalis

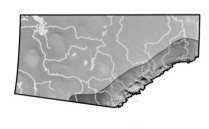

The patterns of the Brook Trout are unique and it is hard to confuse it with any other species. The vermiculations, or "worm tracks," on its back sets this fish apart in Alberta's waters. • Brook Trout were introduced to western Alberta around 1903 from their native range in eastern North America. Since then, this species has spread widely in this part of the province. Its ability to tolerate a wide range of conditions has helped in this dispersal. It prefers cold, slow-moving water but can live in small lakes that are low in oxygen, even beaver ponds. Brook Trout are opportunistic feeders, often waiting under overhanging bushes and near rocks to snap at food drifting by. • Brook Trout are very effective breeders, and many populations overcrowd their habitat. As a result of competition for resources, some Brook Trout stay small and die younger than usual. Where overcrowding of Brook Trout occurs, competition and hybridization by this introduced species can also be a serious problem for the native Bull Trout.

VIEWING TIPS: The best viewing is in autumn when this tiny char comes into foothill and mountain river shallows to spawn in clear, cold water. Some great places to visit around this time are along the Icefields Parkway, in the small channels of the Sunwapta and upper Athabasca rivers (especially near Beauty Creek) and at the outlet of Maligne Lake in Jasper National Park. Carefully walk beside river back channels and spring-fed tributaries.

Spawning Brookies will be working over tiny redds that resemble elk hoof-prints more than they do the big craters that Brown Trout and Bull Trout produce. Sit quietly, watching with close-focusing binoculars. The spawning colours of these fish are magnificent, their orange red bellies highlighted with strong black outlines. Males develop tiny hooked jaws (kypes), like their big Pacific salmon relatives, but on a miniature scale. Combined with the spectacular scenery of an Alberta mountain autumn, this fishwatching experience can be truly wonderful. • In winter, you can also peer through ice-fishing holes at Chickakoo Lake near Stony Plain to see brightly coloured adults.

FEEDING: feeds on aquatic and terrestrial invertebrates, fishes, frogs, snakes and fish eggs and young, even of its own species.

SPAWNING: September to November; usually over gravel beds of shallow streams or lakeshores; male arrives first on spawning grounds and defines a territory; female builds redd up to 20 cm deep over two days; eggs hatch as early as February; mature at one and a half to three years; live up to six years in streams (live to a few years older in lakes).

OTHER NAMES: Eastern Brook Trout, Speckled Trout, Mud Trout, Spotted Trout, Speckled Char, Brook Char, Squaretail, Brookie, Aurora Trout, Mountain Trout.

STATUS: common; introduced.

HABITAT: more versatile than many trout species; in creeks, rivers, mountain lakes, beaver ponds and clear shallow areas of lakes; likes cover underneath banks, under overhanging bushes and behind rocks.

DID YOU KNOW? The Brook Trout is the only char in Alberta to have "jelly donuts" (red or yellow dots with blue halos) on its side. The other fish with jelly donuts is the Brown Trout, which is a true trout, having a light body with black spots.

ID: olive green to dark brown back; silvery white underparts; **"worm tracks" (vermiculations) on top part of body;** flanks with red to yellow tinge; light spots throughout including head; **blue halos around red and yellow dots on sides;** paired fins with white leading edge followed by a black line; squared caudal fin. *Spawning male:* bright red belly.

SIMILAR SPECIES: *Lake Trout* (p. 130): usually larger; whitish spots cover entire body; forked caudal fin. *Bull Trout* (p. 126): no spots on dorsal fin; white leading edge on paired fins not followed by black line; white to pinkish spots; upper jaw extends to eye and turns downward.

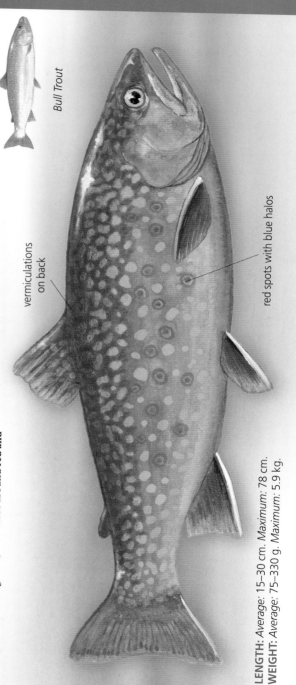

Lake Trout

Bull Trout

vermiculations on back

red spots with blue halos

LENGTH: *Average:* 15–30 cm. *Maximum:* 78 cm.
WEIGHT: *Average:* 75–330 g. *Maximum:* 5.9 kg.

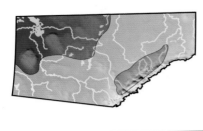

LAKE TROUT   *Salvelinus namaycush*

Lake Trout can become very old and large despite their slow growth. They are the largest species in their family in Alberta, surpassed only by the Chinook Salmon of the West Coast. Lake Trout generally live to about 20 to 25 years of age, but one Lake Trout was found to be 62 years old! These fish mature late in life and may spawn only once every two to three years. This characteristic makes it very difficult for Lake Trout to recover from overfishing. A healthy population was present in Lesser Slave Lake, but it disappeared in the 1920s because of the commercial harvest at the time of the early railway and exploration routes, when human populations around the lake were larger than they are today. • One of the slowest-growing salmonid populations in the country is that of Lake Trout from a cold alpine lake in Jasper National Park's backcountry. A fish from this population was recorded at 28 years old and only 33 cm long! These little Lakers have only about two months of ice-free summer to fatten up on mosquito larvae.

VIEWING TIPS: For most of the year, this deepwater resident is unavailable for fishwatching (unless attached to a fishing line). In autumn, the spawning urge brings them into shallows where diligent fish-lovers can observe their graceful forms. Good places to look for them include Cold River around the outflow from Cold Lake, Swan Lake near Rocky Mountain House, Rock Lake northwest of Hinton and Lake Minnewanka in Banff. Spawning is nocturnal and the best chance to see Lake Trout is in the early morning when the water is calm and the fish are still in the shallows after their

nights' activities. Canoe quietly along the shoreline and watch for long, greyish fish with pale white leading edges on their pectoral and pelvic fins. To overhead fishwatchers, the lines on the fins show up very well, sometimes better than the fish themselves. Because the preferred habitat for Lake Trout is clear water, skin divers (if they are willing to brave the ice-cold waters of an Alberta lake in autumn) can get great views of Lake Trout as they gather near rubble beaches, stream mouths or along reef margins.

FEEDING: adults are piscivorous and take a variety of fishes, particularly whitefishes and sculpins; young fish feed first on zooplankton, then on shrimp and aquatic insects.

SPAWNING: mid-September to October; spawn in water that is 8–11° C, usually in water less than 12 m deep over boulders or gravel; no nest; eggs hatch after 4–5 months; mature at 5–10 years, older as you go north; generally live up to 25 years.

OTHER NAMES: Laker, Mackinaw, Great Lakes Trout, Great Lakes Char, Salmon Trout, Landlocked Salmon, Gray Trout, Great Gray Trout, Mountain Trout, Togue, Namaycush, Masamacush, Forktail.

DID YOU KNOW? In 1961, a 46 kg Lake Trout was pulled up by a gill net on the Saskatchewan side of Lake Athabasca.

STATUS: locally common; sensitive.

HABITAT: deep, cold lakes; may use the surface of lakes in spring and autumn but usually remains below 15 m when surface water temperatures warm to around 10° C.

Brook Trout

ID: generally dark grey on back and sides, paler ventrally; head and body are covered with **whitish irregular spots;** slightly orangish lower fins with white leading edges; **forked caudal fin.** *Juvenile:* 5–12 dark, irregular parr marks along lateral line.

SIMILAR SPECIES: *Brook Trout* (p. 128): "worm tracks" on dorsal area; beige spots and reddish spots surrounded by a blue halo on flanks; dorsal fin has distinct black markings; red belly; caudal fin only slightly forked.

white spots throughout body

forked caudal fin

LENGTH: *Average:* 45–65 cm. *Maximum:* 1 m.
WEIGHT: *Average:* 1–3 kg. *Maximum:* 24 kg.

STATUS: common; secure.

HABITAT: deep water most of the year except during spawning; feeds above rocky or sometimes sandy substrate; hides under rocks when feeding in the shallows.

TROUT-PERCH

Percopsis omiscomaycus

Identification of the Trout-perch should be relatively easy—it is one of only two non-salmonids with an adipose fin in the province (the other is the Stonecat). It also has one row of dark spots along its back and two rows on each side; the most conspicuous row of spots is the lowest, along the lateral line. • Excluding the Rockies, Trout-perch are found in all of Alberta's larger lakes and slower rivers, but populations may be decreasing because of the damming of large rivers. Their favourite hangouts include the deeper parts of water bodies and the nooks under rocks where they can hide from predators. Trout-perch usually feed at night, which is the safest time to be in the shallows. • Very little is known about the Trout-perch in this province, except that it is an important prey species for many piscivorous fishes. Deepwater fishes, including Lake Trout and Burbot, benefit from smaller fishes such as Trout-perch—when a deepwater fish preys on a Trout-perch it absorbs all of the nutrients that the Trout-perch gathered when feeding at the water's surface.

VIEWING TIPS: The Trout-perch is one of the few deepwater fishes that shorebound observers might actually glimpse. Pick a calm evening on the sandy shoreline of a deep Alberta lake (Gregoire Lake, Cold Lake and Lesser Slave Lake are good places). In the dark of a June night, shine a flashlight in the shallow water along the shore. At this time of year, they rise from the depths for their annual spawning. Big eyes and chunky pale bodies are

your best field marks for identifying Trout-perch in the water. Small schools of fat little fish will slowly move along the coarser sand and fine gravel just off shore. You have to stay up late for this fishwatching experience, but it's a fine one.

FEEDING: nocturnal; possibly migrates to shallows to forage on the surface; eats zooplankton, crustaceans, aquatic insects and smaller fishes.

SPAWNING: May to August; breeds only once before dying; may migrate to shore in lakes or up smaller tributaries; spawns above gravel or sandbars; female is surrounded by 2–3 males who press against her sides until she releases her eggs; 3000–5000 eggs per female; then all males release milt as the fertilized eggs float down to stick to the bottom; eggs hatch in 5–8 days; mature after the first year; live from 4–6 years.

OTHER NAMES: Silver Chub.

DID YOU KNOW? A fascinating attribute of this fish is its transparent skin: you can peer straight through to the body cavity if you look at its head carefully. If you look at its head you can actually see the two huge otoliths (ear bones) lying alongside the brain. It is a great fish for pretending you have x-ray vision!

ID: olive to brown on back, lighter on belly; **five lines of spots** run horizontally along body, one line along dorsal line and two lines on each side; lowest rows extend along lateral line and have the darkest spots; **large, triangular head; large eyes;** slightly subterminal mouth; dorsal fin with soft rays, only a few weak spines in both dorsal and anal fins; **adipose fin;** deeply forked caudal fin.

SIMILAR SPECIES: *Logperch* (p. 150): darker and more random spots and patches; two dorsal fins with lines of horizontal spots; smaller, more conical head; no adipose fin. *Iowa Darter* (p. 148): smaller body; squared caudal fin; two dorsal fins of equal size; no adipose fin; may have pinkish markings.

Logperch

Iowa Darter

large head and eyes

five lines of spots run along body

adipose fin

LENGTH: *Average:* 7.5–10 cm. *Maximum:* 13 cm.

BURBOT   *Lota lota*

STATUS: common; secure.

HABITAT: cold lakes and rivers, near the bottom; likes to hide around boulders.

This fish has a ravenous appetite for whitefishes, ciscoes and perches and has been nicknamed "Lawyer" because of its extra sliminess, owing to its thick mucus covering and ability to wiggle out of tight spots. • The Burbot was and still is eaten by people in the North, especially in Siberia, where its skin has even been put to use as a window replacement. • A single barbel hangs from the Burbot's "chin" and one barbel also hangs from each side of the nares. As well, the Burbot's pelvic fins are in front of its pectoral fins. The barbels and the pelvic fins contain taste buds, allowing the Burbot to find and taste its food before popping it into its mouth. • Spawning occurs under the privacy of ice cover, but Burbot do not seem shy about the whole process. Up to a dozen Burbot will gather to participate in a communal love-fest, simultaneously broadcasting eggs and milt in one large wriggling session. • Burbot differ from the rest of Alberta's fishes in that they grow faster in the winter once they hit maturity, but the rate of growth after they have matured is slow and barely noticeable.

VIEWING TIPS: Young Burbot that are 10–20 cm long can often be found along rocky shorelines and in tiny streams near large lakes and rivers, especially in late summer and early autumn. Lac Ste. Anne, Touchwood Lake, Cold Lake and Calling Lake are good places to look for them. Flip over large rocks and logs to see these extremely cute little cods. They look like big tadpoles at first glance and are easily scooped up by hand (make sure you don't have bug spray on your hands!) or with a small dip net. Replace the little cod along with the rock or log when you're finished oohing and awhing over its special beauty. • Large adult Burbot are often observed by ice fishers in late winter. When you peer down a darkened ice-fishing hole over a shallow, sandy lake-bottom, you might see individual Burbot slowly swimming along, or a cluster of swarming, mating fish might swirl on past.

FEEDING: adults eat mostly fishes but also molluscs, crustaceans and whitefish eggs; juveniles feed on aquatic insects and insect larvae and become more piscivorous as they mature.

SPAWNING: from February to March, under ice; over sand or gravel; groups of Burbot gather together to simultaneously release eggs and milt; no nest or parental care; hatch in 30 days; mature at 3–4 years; live to 15 years.

OTHER NAMES: Eelpout, Lawyer, Methy, Maria, Loche, Freshwater Cod, Sandling, Dogfish, Spineless Cat, Mudblower, Mother-of-eels, Gudgeon, Cuskfish.

DID YOU KNOW? *Lota lota* could describe the amount of dorsal or anal fin on the Burbot, but *lota* is actually a form of the 16th-century French word for this fish, *Lotte*. The common name also comes from Old French; *Burbotte* means to wallow in mud.

ID: long, round body; scales barely visible; long, pointed head; small eyes; terminal mouth; **barbel on "chin"; one barbel from each nare;** all fins are soft rayed; first dorsal fin is short, **second dorsal fin is elongated, almost touching caudal fin; anal fin similar to second dorsal fin;** caudal fin and pectoral fins are rounded; pelvic fins are positioned in front of pectorals and are small and pointed downward; dark brown to yellow with dark mottling along entire body.

SIMILAR SPECIES: *Stonecat* (p. 100): eight barbels surround mouth; large, rounded first dorsal fin; second dorsal fin is half as long as Burbot's; rectangular caudal fin surrounds caudal peduncle; found only in the Milk River.

Stonecat

one barbel on "chin" and one barbel from each nare

second dorsal fin equal to anal fin

rounded dorsal fin

LENGTH: *Average:* 40–60 cm. *Maximum:* 1 m.
WEIGHT: *Average:* 2–3 kg. *Maximum:* 8.6 kg.

BROOK STICKLEBACK   *Culaea inconstans*

These little stickleback are able to live in a range of conditions from the coldest waters of northern Alberta to the saline potholes of the prairies. They will often take the first opportunity to disperse, even into a farmer's flooded field that may eventually leave them high and dry. They are tolerant of low oxygen, and they can even survive in small pools in winter by using the oxygen-rich water that surrounds trapped gas bubbles. These little fish have even been found in artesian wells, which indicates that they are present even in underground streams! • When you're trying to find Brookies, look near the edges of a water body that has plenty of vegetation. If you happen upon a pond with a high density of Brook Stickleback you may be lucky enough to see a "food fight" —if food is scarce, an individual fish will try to tear food from another fish's mouth. If times are really tough, this stickleback may even burrow into the mud in search of invertebrates. • Muskrats, shrews, salamanders, grebes, predaceous insects, fishes and snakes all eat Brook Stickleback. Many of these animals may think twice about their next Brookie snack when they learn that up to a third of the body weight of some Brook Stickleback can be attributed to *Schistocephalus*, a larval tapeworm. Eew!

VIEWING TIPS: Brook Stickleback can be seen in the most amazing places: sluggish streams that look stagnant, roadside ditches and almost-dry beaver ponds. A good time to go stickleback-catching is in the spring, when runoff swells small streams. A small, aquarium-style dip net duct-taped to a willow pole makes for an ideal stickleback-catcher. Walk along a stream bank, watching for small minnowlike fish hovering in one spot. With a quick scoop, you can catch these little gems. Take a moment or two to admire the cool-looking spiny fins, wasp-waist tail, and so-tiny mouth. Always return the fish back to the water quickly, but this species is hardy enough to withstand a bit of curious kid-handling. • Later in the summer, it's great to find a stickleback near its nest and watch the hover-dart movements as it clears tiny bits of weeds or attacks a marauding plankton. Some good Alberta viewing sites for Brookies are ravine streams in Edmonton and Calgary, Beaverhill Lake and Astotin Lake in Elk Island National Park.

FEEDING: eats aquatic invertebrates and their larvae, crustaceans, very small fish eggs and juvenile fishes, even of its own species.

SPAWNING: May to July; spawns in areas with aquatic vegetation; male defends a territory and builds an oval-shaped nest with vegetation and his own kidney secretions; female is wooed or pushed into a male's territory; he pokes his nose into her abdomen area to induce the release of eggs into the nest; female exits through the bottom of the nest, which the male must then repair; female mates every three days for a month, releasing about 2000 eggs in total; male defends eggs and aerates them until they hatch in about 21 days; mature in first year; live to four years.

STATUS: common; secure.

HABITAT: almost anywhere, including ponds, creeks, saline sloughs, rivers and lake edges.

OTHER NAMES: Common Stickleback, Black Stickleback, Pinfish, Five-spined Stickleback.

DID YOU KNOW? Many of Alberta's Brook Stickleback populations include individuals that are missing the two pelvic spines that normally occur on this species. This characteristic may be an adaptation to a lack of predators in some ponds.

ID: mouth terminal or supraterminal; **4–6 dorsal spines; two pelvic spines; origin of anal fin is equal with origin of dorsal fin; anal and dorsal fins positioned near tail;** thin caudal peduncle; rounded caudal fin; dark brown to olive with mottling on back and sides; beige belly. *Spawning male:* black bands through eyes; very dark overall. *Spawning female:* varied and splotchy colours.

SIMILAR SPECIES: *Ninespine Stickleback* (p. 138): from 9–11 dorsal spines that alternate leaning left and right; thinner caudal peduncle; found in Beaver River drainage basin and northern Alberta. *Threespine Stickleback:* three dorsal spines of unequal length, first two spines are large, third spine is smaller; bony plate in pectoral area; located only in Hasse Lake and in storm ponds around Edmonton.

Ninespine Stickleback

4–6 dorsal spines

dorsal fin equal to anal fin

LENGTH: *Average:* 5 cm. *Maximum:* 9 cm.

NINESPINE STICKLEBACK   *Pungitius pungitius*

STATUS: locally common; undetermined status.

HABITAT: cold lakes and rivers.

In early April, the bellies of male Ninespine Stickleback blush red, signaling the beginning of the spawning season. Grabbing loose, floating vegetation, a male will find a spot heavy with aquatic vegetation and weave his nesting material around underwater stems to create a tunnel-shaped nest. He "glues" the nest together with a secretion from his kidney. His next priority is finding a female to fill the nest with small yellow eggs, which he will then fertilize and ferociously guard. The female does not contribute at all to the rearing of the young, which hatch after 6–12 days and stay around the nest for up to a month. While cleaning the eggs with his mouth, the single dad Ninespine may swallow one of his youngsters. • Ninespine Stickleback can have from 7–11 spines on their backs. Their spines alternate between leaning left and leaning right, unlike those of other sticklebacks. If you don't feel like you can identify this species based on its spines, then take a look at the caudal peduncle. It is much skinnier than the caudal peduncles of the other two sticklebacks and looks like someone has come along and pinched it. • In behaviour and general appearance, this fish is similar to our more common Brook Stickleback. Unlike the Brook Stickleback, however, it is found on the Barren Grounds and along the Arctic Coast, sometimes living in almost permanently frozen tundra ponds for most of its short life.

VIEWING TIPS: Ninespines are great to watch as they hover, with vibrating dorsal fins, above the bottom of a sluggish boreal forest stream or along the shore of a deep, cold lake. You may see one suddenly dart forward to nail an unsuspecting *Daphnia* (water flea). Because they don't dash madly about like many of our other small fishes, Ninespines are a fine species for quiet observation of fish behaviour and social structure. Cold Lake, Amisk Lake and Amisk River are good places to look for these charismatic little fish. Marie Creek, near the bridge on Highway 897 west of Cold Lake, is also a good place to try in June and July.

FEEDING: eats plankton, aquatic insects, crustaceans and fish eggs and larvae, even of its own species.

SPAWNING: May to July; male prefers to build nest in an area with thick aquatic vegetation; floating debris, such as grass and twigs, are woven into a tunnel shape attached to vegetation; female deposits eggs into the nest; male defends the nest and young; eggs hatch in 6–12 days; young stay near the nest for about a month; mature in first year; live up to four years.

OTHER NAMES: Nine-spined Stickleback, Ten-spine Stickleback, Stickleback, Pinfish, Tiny Burnstickle.

DID YOU KNOW? *Pungitius* means "pricking" in Latin.

Brook Stickleback

ID: slender-bodied; terminal mouth; **7–11 dorsal spines, alternating left to right; origin of anal fin is equal with origin of dorsal fin;** dorsal and anal fins positioned near tail; caudal peduncle very thin; squared caudal fin; greyish green dorsally with black mottling on silver sides; whitish belly. *Spawning male:* red blush on belly.

SIMILAR SPECIES: *Brook Stickleback* (p. 136): five spines on back are in a straight line; thicker caudal peduncle. *Threespine Stickleback:* two large spines on back, third spine is small and near dorsal fin; thicker caudal peduncle; "armour" on underside of pectoral area.

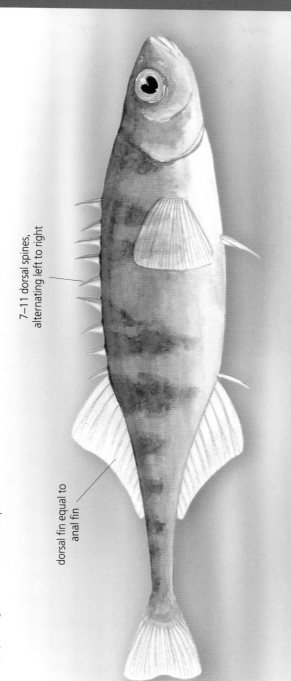

7–11 dorsal spines, alternating left to right

dorsal fin equal to anal fin

LENGTH: *Average:* 5 cm. *Maximum:* 7 cm.

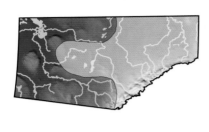

SLIMY SCULPIN   *Cottus cognatus*

From above, the Slimy Sculpin looks like an arrow: its large pointed head tapers to a thin tail. A closer look reveals fanlike pectoral fins and a bullish face. • Members of the sculpin family are masters of camouflage; dark mottling on their grey bodies blend in perfectly with the gravelly bottoms that they frequent. Most of their movement occurs at night, feeding on bottom-dwelling invertebrates and chasing after insect and fish larvae. During the day Slimies remain still under rocky hideouts, avoiding Northern Pike, Lake Trout, Burbot and other predators. • In late spring, males clean out small territories. Challengers that arrive are met with short, quick charges in their direction until the loser retreats, his breeding colours fading with his withdrawal. Females are welcomed into the territory, where they deposit their eggs on the "ceiling" of the nest, under the well-guarded rocks. More than one female may visit a nest, and the male will guard his territory for up to five weeks. • Slimies have the most adventurous past of any of the sculpins—they are relics of the last ice age. Imagine these little tadpoles scooting out of the way as a woolly mammoth wades in a shallow tundra pond, or imagine a little school of Slimies picking bits of meat from a saber-tooth cat's latest kill along a Pleistocene riverbank.

VIEWING TIPS: Slimy Sculpin are rarely noticed by fishwatchers. Their excellent camouflage means that you see nothing, then suddenly, in a puff of silt and a flash of motion, this magician of the silt disappears into a rocky hideaway. It's well worth wading around in the rocky shallows of northern rivers or lakes to search for this fish. Cold Lake, clear streams around Fort McMurray (try the House River and Hangingstone River on Highway 63) and Smoky River are good places to look for Slimies.

FEEDING: eats crustaceans, aquatic insects, small fishes and occasionally detritus.

SPAWNING: May to June; male cleans and defends a small, rocky territory; female enters the territory and he presses her up to the ceiling of the nest, where she deposits up to 1400 eggs; male guards the nest before and after hatching; eggs hatch after four weeks; mature at 3–4 years; live to seven years.

OTHER NAMES: Cottus Big Fin, Stargazer, Northern Sculpin, Slimy Muddler, Miller's Thumb.

DID YOU KNOW? This northern fish is found in both North America and Asia, as well as on an island between the two continents, the St. Lawrence Island in the Bering Strait. In fact, the range of this sculpin provides evidence of the long-ago existence of the Bering land bridge, which many scientists believe was the primary route over which Asian animals dispersed to North America during the ice ages.

STATUS: common; secure.

HABITAT: boreal rivers and large lakes; gravelly or rocky bottoms of cold water bodies.

Shorthead Sculpin

Spoonhead Sculpin

ID: rounded body tapers to tail; no teeth on roof of mouth; **small preopercular ("cheek") spine points straight backward;** terminal mouth; large pectoral fins with dark lines along spines; dorsal fins touch; first dorsal fin is small; **second dorsal fin is long (15–19 rays),** almost to caudal fin; anal fin has long spines; pelvic fins are long with 2–3 rays; squared caudal fin has dark lines; brown to light grey body with dark mottling; whitish ventrally. *Spawning male:* darker colours on body; outline of first dorsal fin is orange.

SIMILAR SPECIES: *Shorthead Sculpin* (p. 142): on average, a few more soft rays on anal fin. *Spoonhead Sculpin* (p. 144): flat, wide head; preopercular ("cheek") spine curves strongly upward; lateral line extends along caudal peduncle; evident prickles along most of body.

small preopercular spine points straight back

15–19 rays in second dorsal fin

LENGTH: *Average:* 6 cm. *Maximum:* 9 cm.

SHORTHEAD SCULPIN *Cottus confusus*

As it swims around southern Alberta, the Shorthead Sculpin is oblivious to the confusion it is causing ichthyologists. This sculpin usually occurs in fast, cold water, such as the Columbia River drainage basin or Montana's cool streams. The slow, relatively warm, silty water of the Milk River seems the opposite of its usual habitat, but most Shorthead Sculpin that inhabit southern Alberta match up with the rest of the North American population. • Biologists are trying to determine if the more robust fish from the Oldman River drainage basin and the fish from the Milk River are the same subspecies. Some biologists even believe that the sculpin found in the Oldman River drainage basin should be considered an entirely different species, the Mottled Sculpin. Only time will tell, though, and until then the Shorthead Sculpin remains the only sculpin in the extreme south of the province. • *Cottus* comes from an older name for the common European Sculpin, and *confusus* is an appropriate species name.

VIEWING TIPS: Because this fish is found in prairie rivers, viewing opportunities depend on the colour of the water. In autumn, low water often means clear water, and it's a lot more pleasant in Alberta's south country when the summer heat has faded. Try looking for Shorthead Sculpin in the Milk River, upstream of Writing-On-Stone Provincial Park, and in the St. Mary River, southwest of Cardston. Watch carefully around rocky, rubble areas. Like other sculpins, Shorteads are masters of camouflage. You may even spot the slow movement of their gill covers before you see the entire fish. Use good polarized sunglasses and be patient. Slowly wading and flushing the sculpins ahead of you sometimes works, too.

FEEDING: benthic feeder; eats small aquatic invertebrates.

SPAWNING: May; male defends a rocky territory; female deposits eggs underneath the surface of rocks; she releases up to 250 eggs per spawning season; eggs hatch in 3–4 weeks; mature in 2–3 years; live up to seven years.

OTHER NAMES: none.

DID YOU KNOW? All sculpins lack a swim bladder and for good reason—they spend almost all of their time camouflaged near the bottom of water bodies and do not need to float up and down the water column.

STATUS: uncommon; may be at risk.

HABITAT: usually frequents fast, cold streams; in Alberta it is also is found in the Milk River, which is silty and slow; needs rocks for spawning.

ID: rounded body tapers to tail; **thick, round head;** teeth on roof of mouth; **small preopercular ("cheek") spine points straight backward;** terminal mouth; large pectoral fins; dorsal fins touch; first dorsal fin is small; **second dorsal fin is long (11–15 rays),** almost to squared caudal fin; brown to light grey body with irregular mottling.

SIMILAR SPECIES: *Slimy Sculpin* (p. 140): more rounded head; thinner body in comparison to size of head; no teeth on roof of mouth. *Spoonhead Sculpin* (p. 144): long upward-curved spine on operculum.

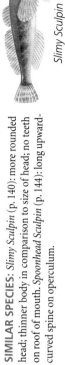

Slimy Sculpin

Spoonhead Sculpin

11–15 rays in second dorsal fin

LENGTH: *Average:* 5–7 cm. *Maximum:* 11 cm.

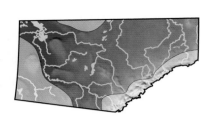

SPOONHEAD SCULPIN   *Cottus ricei*

On the sides of the Spoonhead Sculpin's large, flat head are pairs of preopercular ("cheek") spines, which likely make predators think twice before gulping down these sculpin. One pair of spines is larger than the others, giving the appearance of buffalo horns. Another adaptation to heavy predation is the small prickles that cover the bodies of young Spoonheads, which also help to protect these scaleless fish in their rocky habitat. • The colour of this sculpin becomes darker as you go farther north. In Alberta, the Spoonhead is widely distributed in large rivers and streams and is found in some lakes, primarily in the foothills. Although the Spoonhead Sculpin likes silty waters, it has only one documented occurrence in the Milk River. • The Spoonhead is found almost exclusively within Canada. Although its range is not well known, it seems to follow the retreat of the last glacier sheet, which covered Canada and carved deep lakes and rivers in its wake. • Sculpins are the fishes that fly fishers try to imitate when they tie a very popular trout fly called the "Muddler Minnow."

VIEWING TIPS: The best places to look for this fish are in the Brown Trout streams of west-central Alberta (such as Stauffer Creek, Shunda Creek and Tay River) as well as in the McLeod River. Because they're mainly nocturnal, you generally have to search for these sculpin under rocks. In clear, foothill rivers, slowly lift up head-sized rocks that aren't cemented to the bottom with silt. Sculpins hiding under these boulders will sometimes sit still long enough for you to have a good look. Gently replace the stone, as the underside may be the nest-rock that the sculpin is defending. Try to refrain from lifting rocks during the time of actual spawning. If the sculpin darts away, keep a careful watch, because it usually just moves a metre or so and hides under another stone.

FEEDING: nocturnal benthic feeder; eats aquatic insects and benthic invertebrates, such as molluscs.

SPAWNING: late summer to early autumn; male defends a rocky territory; female places up to 1200 orangish eggs underneath rocks; male chases away female after she has spawned and allows other females to spawn in his nest; after he fertilizes the eggs he aerates them with his pectoral fins and guards them until they hatch in 2–3 weeks; mature in 2–3 years; live to six years.

OTHER NAMES: Cow-faced Sculpin, Muddler.

DID YOU KNOW? The pre-eminent Alberta sculpin-lover and expert, Wayne Roberts, has added much to our knowledge of the spawning and general behaviour of the species in this delightful and taxonomically confusing family of native fishes.

STATUS: uncommon; may be at risk.

HABITAT: among rocks in rivers, streams and lakeshores; also in deeper lake waters.

ID: flat, wide head tapers to skinny caudal peduncle; **large preopercular ("cheek") spine curves upward and inward;** small, beady eyes; large pelvic fins; two touching dorsal fins; 16–19 rays in second dorsal fin; small, squared caudal fin; dark brown to olive dorsally; colour fades along sides to white belly; dark splotches cover body.

SIMILAR SPECIES: *Slimy Sculpin* (p. 140): rounded head; preopercular spine is short and slightly bent backward; fewer prickles do not cover all of body; lateral line is incomplete.

Slimy Sculpin

flat, wide head

large preopercular spine curves upward

16–19 rays in second dorsal fin

LENGTH: *Average:* 8 cm. *Maximum:* 14 cm.

DEEPWATER SCULPIN *Myoxocephalus thompsoni*

Thousands of years ago, the Deepwater Sculpin was pushed south from its arctic home by advancing glaciers. Once the glaciers receded, populations of this fish remained within some of Canada's deeper lakes. Alberta's Waterton Lake is the only place in Alberta where it is known to occur. • The Deepwater Sculpin was once thought to be the same species as the Fourhorn Sculpin (*M. quadricornis*) of the Great Lakes, but fossil records have proven that the two species have been distinct since before the ice age. • The greatest difference between the Deepwater Sculpin and the rest of Alberta's sculpins is the large gap between its two dorsal fins.

VIEWING TIPS: Unless you hitch a ride on a deepwater submersible, you're not likely to see this tiny denizen of the deep. Occasionally, it has been caught in shallow water, but this ice-age relic calls the dark abyss home. Fishy naturalists at cold, deep lakes should pay close attention to anglers' cleaning tables where Lake Trout may be filleted. This is where Deepwater Sculpin are most often seen, usually when biologists examine trout stomachs. • Waterton Lake is the only place where this fish is confirmed to occur,

so far. If you go fishing for Lake Trout up in the lovely, deep lakes of northern Alberta, watch in the trouts' tummies for tiny fishes with big, oversized heads and fins. If you see one, pop the partially digested little princess into a plastic bag with a good shot of somebody's whiskey and bring it (the fish, not the whiskey) to your local fisheries biologist, who will be absolutely ecstatic to receive even a rotted chunk of Deepwater Sculpin.

FEEDING: usually a benthic feeder; eats crustaceans, aquatic insects, amphipods and fish eggs.

SPAWNING: little is known because of its deepwater habits; summer, perhaps into autumn; mature at 2–3 years; may live to seven years.

OTHER NAMES: Fourhorn Sculpin, Scorpion Fish.

DID YOU KNOW? Deepwater Sculpin (and their predators) can be found in very deep water, indeed. Lake Trout caught at depths of nearly 400 m in Great Bear Lake, Northwest Territories, had Deepwater Sculpin in their stomachs.

STATUS: rare; undetermined status.

HABITAT: deep waters of cold, deep lakes.

ID: mottled colouring; **four preopercular spines; two dorsal fins**, the first spiny and the second fleshy, **with a large gap between them;** large pectoral fins. *Male:* second dorsal fin is enlarged; pelvic and upper caudal rays are enlarged. *Spawning male:* nuptial tubercles on pectoral fins, second dorsal fin and above lateral line.

SIMILAR SPECIES: *Shorthead Sculpin* (p. 142): only found in the Milk River system; dorsal fins touch.

Shorthead Sculpin

four preopercular spines

large gap between dorsal fins

LENGTH: *Average:* 3–6 cm. *Maximum:* 7 cm.

IOWA DARTER

Etheostoma exile

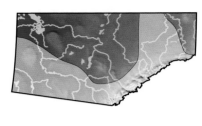

L ike tiny, colourful jewels, Iowa Darters dash about the clear waters of the Alberta's lakes and rivers. These small members of the perch family are indicators of healthy waters, disappearing when the water quality decreases. • If you have sharp eyes, you can watch the Iowa Darter's transparent, decorated fins flutter with the movement of the water, then keep track of this fish as it quickly darts and reappears a few metres away. Its quick movements and habit of hiding under rocks or vegetation makes it difficult for predators to catch. On the off chance that an Iowa Darter is caught, its torn skin cells will release "Scheckstoff," an alarm substance that is usually associated with the minnow family. When other Iowa Darters sense this substance, they know that danger is near and react accordingly.

VIEWING TIPS: Darters look like miniature perches and have brilliant Christmas-tree colours on their dorsal fins. Viewed from above, their darting movements are quite unminnow-like and interesting, but you have to get up close with this fish to really appreciate it. Look for this little gem at Cold Lake, North Buck Lake near Boyle and Wolf Lake near Bonnyville. Snorkel slowly over a sandy bottom, or

use a small seine net and put captured Iowas into a glass jar for a few quick moments. A magnifying glass helps to see the reddish orange dorsal fin, which is offset by stunning turquoise bands and black margins.

FEEDING: benthic and pelagic; eats aquatic invertebrates, insect larvae and plankton.

SPAWNING: May to June; male defends a territory of shallow water among vegetation; female swims above rocks or roots that eggs can stick to; male "mounts" female with his pelvic fins placed on her dorsal fin and his caudal peduncle parallel with hers; he continues to defend his territory after spawning; she mates with other males; she releases 250 eggs per spawning session; eggs hatch within 20 days; mature in 2–3 years; live up to 5 years.

OTHER NAMES: Yellowbelly, Red-sided Darter, Weed Darter.

DID YOU KNOW? *Etheostoma* is Greek for "filter mouth," and *exile* is Latin for "slim."

STATUS: locally common; secure.

HABITAT: clear lakes and streams; near the bottom and around vegetation.

ID: small, slender body; **anal fin smaller than second dorsal fin;** dark "teardrop" under eye; mouth just barely subterminal; two dorsal fins, first is red, black and spiny, second is fleshy and transparent with black markings; rest of fins are transparent with dark markings; **squared caudal fin;** olive green or brown dorsally and ventrally; whitish belly. *Spawning male:* dark red, blue and black markings on sides.

SIMILAR SPECIES: *Logperch* (p. 150): larger and longer body; darker dorsally; dorsal fins longer, connected and not as colourful; cone-shaped head.

Logperch

squared caudal fin

anal fin smaller than second dorsal fin

LENGTH: *Average:* 4–5 cm. *Maximum:* 6 cm. Females are larger than males.

LOGPERCH *Percina caprodes*

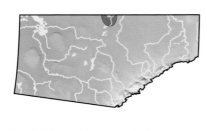

STATUS: locally uncommon; undetermined status.

HABITAT: cool lakes and rivers; prefers gravel or sandy bottoms.

Alberta contains the most western population of Logperch in Canada, and even in our province, this fish only occurs in lakes and rivers of the lower Beaver River drainage basin. • Because the Logperch is larger than the Iowa Darter but smaller than the Yellow Perch, its genus name is *Percina*, which means "little perch." *Caprodes* means "piglike" and refers to the protruding upper jaw of the Logperch. The fish uses its "big nose" to flip over rocks or debris in search of invertebrates. • Logperch usually remain in water deeper than 1 m, but they come into shallow water during the spawning season, when large gangs of males gather at their respective tributaries or lakeshores to prowl for mates. Competition is fierce, because usually one or two females at a time will join the group. Males with less spawning prowess can still exact revenge on the more lucky males by eating their fertilized eggs. Larvae that hatch in a stream must float helplessly to still water before they can start to feed on zooplankton, leaving them vulnerable to predators, including belted kingfishers.

VIEWING TIPS: The best places to look for these fish are at Cold Lake (right in front of town by the marina or along the shore at Long Bay Provincial Park), Marie Lake and Wolf Lake. They will likely be sitting motionless on the gravelly bottom. It is best to look in autumn or spring, when the water is cool and these fish may be in shallower water than normal. They look somewhat like the very common Iowa Darter, but are much darker and "funkier"—they stick out like a punk rocker at a formal dance. Logperch are fairly rare in Alberta, so you get good bragging rights if you see one. Fish-lovers are usually also general nature-lovers, and an autumn trip to the country around Cold Lake is great for birdwatching, tree-colour watching, and all-around spectacular natural history.

FEEDING: uses its large snout to turn over detritus and rocks; eats invertebrates, including insect larvae and crustaceans, and fish eggs.

SPAWNING: June; a large group of males concentrates near gravel or sandy lakeshores or up small tributaries; a female swims through the group and stops near the bottom; one male settles on her back and clasps her with his pectoral fins and tail; no nest or parental care; eggs are covered in bottom substrate with spawning action; a female releases 10–20 eggs per spawning session to a total of about 2000 eggs per season; mature after the first year; live to four years.

OTHER NAMES: Zebrafish, Darter, Hogfish, Rockfish.

DID YOU KNOW? The Logperch is one of two darters that live in Alberta. Darters are known only to North America, and the Logperch has the widest distribution of any of them—it extends east to Québec and south to Texas.

ID: 15–20 black bands along greyish body; anal fin is same size as second dorsal fin; dark "teardrop" under each eye; pointed, flat head; "cheeks" and operculum are scaled; **subterminal mouth;** all fins are transparent; first dorsal fin has spines and orange and black stripes; dark spot between caudal peduncle and caudal fin. *Spawning male:* yellowish colour on body becomes more intense; develops nuptial tubercles on belly and pectoral fins.

SIMILAR SPECIES: *Iowa Darter* (p. 148): smaller; sometimes has pinkish hue to body; barely subterminal mouth; rounded head; fewer rays on fins; caudal fin more square; spawning males have alternating blue and red blotches on sides.

Iowa Darter

subterminal mouth

anal fin equal in size to second dorsal fin

LENGTH: *Average:* 7–9 cm. *Maximum:* 10 cm.

YELLOW PERCH

Perca flavescens

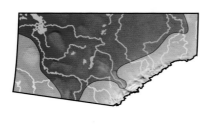

The deep-bodied, slow-moving Yellow Perch adds some much-needed colour to Alberta's lakes in winter. Its recognizable black saddles have earned it nicknames such as "Raccoon Perch" and "Bandit Fish." • This common perch is a prey species for almost every piscivorous predator in Alberta—even whitefishes have been found with Yellow Perch in their stomachs. To escape from predators, young Yellow Perch hide in the vegetated shallows of lakes. If they escape the hungry mouths of Northern Pike and great blue herons, the now larger fish graduate to deeper waters, only to face new predators, such as Lake Trout and Walleye. Yellow Perch can get their revenge, however. Studies in Ontario have shown that if Walleye are overfished and reduced in numbers, Yellow Perch will increase and feed heavily on young Northern Pike! • Young Yellow Perch swim in schools, and they join similar-sized Spottail Shiners when given the chance. Predators seem to prey on the Spottails before the Yellow Perch. • For a long time the Yellow Perch has been a regular catch for local anglers and ice fishers, but recently anglers have been complaining of a major decline in the most popular perch fisheries. This species is particularly vulnerable to the effects of overfishing because it grows so slowly—any Yellow Perch longer than 30 cm is at least 10 years old.

VIEWING TIPS: These perch can provide you with hours of enjoyable fishwatching. On sunny summer days, you can lean over the side of the boat and watch schools of Yellow Perch hunt for tasty water bugs and hide from their classic enemy, the barracuda-like Northern Pike. Young are easily caught in small seines and are hardy enough for a few moments of examination in the hand. Moose Lake, by Bonnyville, and Pine Lake, near Wetaskiwin, are good sites for watching perch. • Snorkelling works well for perch-watching, because these fish are often in the warm shallows and don't dash away like trouts. Twin Lakes, west of Pigeon Lake, offers very clear water and excellent snorkelling. • In winter, it's great fun to watch Yellow Perch through ice-fishing holes or, even better, using the increasingly common and affordable underwater video cameras that can be lowered down through ice holes.

FEEDING: adults eat smaller fish larvae, smaller fishes, crayfish, leeches and molluscs; young feed on zooplankton and aquatic insect larvae.

SPAWNING: early spring after break-up; shallow, sheltered, vegetated areas in tributaries; one female is flanked by two or more males; eggs are released in sticky strings and draped over vegetation or rocks while fertilized (an excellent strategy to keep the precious eggs away from the suffocating silt on the lake bottom); no parental care; eggs hatch in 14 days; males mature in 3–5 years; females mature in 4–6 years; live to 15 years or more.

OTHER NAMES: Bandit Fish, Convict, Ringed Perch, Raccoon Perch, Jack Perch.

STATUS: common; vulnerable to overfishing.

HABITAT: common in lakes and less common in rivers; young stay in weeds off shorelines; older fish inhabit deeper waters.

Walleye

6–7 large, black saddles

face looks upturned

DID YOU KNOW? *Flavescens* is Latin for "becoming yellow or gold," referring to the change of colour from olive on the Yellow Perch's back to yellow down its sides.

ID: deep body; dark green dorsally; **yellow on flanks with 6–7 vertical black saddles;** white belly; small head; **face looks upturned** as if the fish is craning its neck; large rise on neck; two dorsal fins, first is spiny, second is fleshy; pelvic fin origins close together; slightly indented caudal fin.

SIMILAR SPECIES: *Walleye* (p. 156): larger; shallower body; black and gold flecks cover body; white tip to bottom of caudal fin; glassy eye.

LENGTH: *Average:* 20–25 cm. *Maximum:* 39 cm.
WEIGHT: *Average:* 200–300 g. *Maximum:* 1.4 kg.

SAUGER   *Stizostedion canadense*

Most anglers who find a Sauger on the end of their line believe they have caught an immature Walleye, because in general, the similar-looking Sauger is smaller than the Walleye. There are a couple of good ways to tell the two apart. The Walleye's first dorsal fin does not have distinct dark spots like the Sauger's does. The Walleye sports only two distinct spots: a black one at the back end of the first dorsal fin and a white one on the very bottom tip of the caudal fin. There is also a physiological difference between the two species: the Sauger is better adapted to silty waters and has better eyesight than its close relative (most of the Sauger's food is hunted by sight). Sauger and Walleye are able to hybridize, resulting in "Saugeye," which can have varied patterns and colours. If all of this leaves you confused, look at the range maps and consider the habitat. In Alberta, Sauger reside only in large turbid rivers such as the North Saskatchewan. In other provinces, including Ontario, Sauger are lake dwellers as well.

VIEWING TIPS: Considering the murky river water that Sauger inhabit, it is lucky for fishwatchers that these fish sometimes hug the shallow shoreline. They can be seen in a few centimetres of water, right at the edge of the North Saskatchewan River. They look like skinny and much darker versions of Walleye. In clear river water (clear water is rare in Alberta prairie rivers, but it happens), their dark saddles

show up well when viewed from the side by snorkellers. Look for them in the North Saskatchewan River, near the Strathcona Science Park in Edmonton, in the Red Deer River, at the Steveville Campground on Highway 876 at the mouth of Berry Creek, and in the Milk River, near Writing-On-Stone Provincial Park.

FEEDING: hunts mostly by sight (its *tapetum lucidum* is even better than that of the Walleye); eats smaller fishes, such as sticklebacks and minnows, and larger invertebrates, including leeches and crustaceans.

SPAWNING: late May to early June; males migrate to smaller tributaries before females; spawning occurs at night; one or more males flank a female; no nest; eggs and milt are broadcast over gravel substrate; eggs are not adhesive but nestle between spaces in gravel; eggs hatch after about a month; spend one week near gravel as larvae; males mature at two years, females mature at 3–4 years; live to 13 years.

OTHER NAMES: Sand Pickerel, Blue Pickerel, Grey Pickerel, Sand Pike, Blue Pike, Grey Pike, Jack Salmon, Horsefish.

DID YOU KNOW? When Sauger rest, they lie right on the bottom. In contrast, Walleye hover just above the bottom.

STATUS: uncommon; sensitive.

HABITAT: large, silty rivers.

ID: rounded in cross-section; **cone-shaped head;** terminal mouth; pelvic fin origin just behind pectoral fin origin; pectoral fins on adults are quite distinctively round, thick and very dark; **first dorsal fin is spiny with rows of dark spots;** second dorsal fin is fleshy with spots less defined; light brown on back, with **3–4 dark, mottled saddles;** white underparts.

SIMILAR SPECIES: *Walleye* (p. 156): usually larger; dark spot at posterior base of first dorsal fin; no distinct spots on the darker first dorsal fin; white spot on lower lobe of caudal fin.

Walleye

rows of dark spots on first dorsal fin

cone-shaped head

LENGTH: *Average:* 30–45 cm. *Maximum:* 66 cm.
WEIGHT: *Average:* 0.5–1 kg. *Maximum:* 2.8 kg.

WALLEYE *Stizostedion vitreum*

When Albertans think of the Walleye, visions of fishing on a hot summer day float into their heads. Over the past hundred or so years, the population of Alberta's most popular sport fish has been through some ups and downs. Prior to the 20th century, the Walleye was one of this province's top fish predators. Unfortunately, overharvesting of this particularly tasty member of the perch family led to the collapse of many Walleye populations in Alberta. Beginning in 1985, Walleye from the Cold Lake Fish Hatchery were stocked in the most severely collapsed lakes. Lakes that had been partially depleted were left to recover, because fish biologists did not want to endanger the natural genetic stock remaining in the lakes. Since then, commercial fishers, sport fishers, biologists and other interest groups have teamed up to create a recovery plan for the Walleye. A large part of the plan focuses on protecting female fish because it takes longer for them to mature (up to nine years) and it is important that they get a chance to spawn before they are caught. The Walleye is now a flagship species for responsible angling practices—many educational programs focus on this great fish. Many Walleye populations have recovered from the heavy overfishing of the 1970s and 1980s, and large runs of these boreal forest aquatic predators are once again making their ecological mark in Alberta.

VIEWING TIPS: On calm, hot summer days, Walleye can often be seen slowly swimming over sandy shallows in northern Alberta lakes—Touchwood Lake has good viewing. Watch for pale forms drifting away from your canoe or boat. The Walleye is easily mistaken for a sucker, but it is a dead giveaway if you look for the stark contrast of the white tip on the lower lobe of the tail fin. ● You can see many Walleye at night during their spring spawning along gravel beaches at places such as Calling Lake or Buck Lake. At the peak of spawning, they swim right up next to shore, often in such shallow water that their dorsal fins are in the air. During May and early June, stop at bridges over small rivers in northeastern Alberta to check for spawning Walleye in the rubble and gravel usually found under the highway bridges. The McLeod River, downstream of Edson, is a good place to go snorkelling and observing river Walleye.

FEEDING: mostly piscivorous; occasionally eats insects.

SPAWNING: April to May; in moderate- to fast-running water or over rocky shoals in lakes; males migrate to spawning area first; spawning occurs at night; female is flanked by one or more males; no nest; female rushes into shallow water and turns on her side to release her eggs; males release milt as the eggs are released; female carries from 20,000–90,000 eggs per season; eggs settle into gravel until they hatch in two and a half to three weeks; males mature at 5–7 years; females mature at 6–9 years; live up to nearly 30 years.

OTHER NAMES: Pickerel, Pike-perch, Wall-eyed Pike.

STATUS: uncommon to common; sensitive to overfishing.

HABITAT: large rivers and relatively deep lakes; prefers low amounts of light.

DID YOU KNOW? This fish gets its name from the term "walleyed," which refers to a bulging of the eyes. The Walleye's large glassy eyes are a result of the *tapetum lucidum*, the reflective membrane at the back of each eye that allows the Walleye to see in dark water.

ID: cone-shaped head; **large, glassy eyes; two dorsal fins—first is spiny, second is fleshy; back end of first dorsal fin has a dark spot at base; tip of anal fin is white;** caudal fin is forked; **white spot on end of lower lobe of caudal fin;** large, terminal mouth with many teeth; dark back, with black and gold flecks on body; white underparts.

SIMILAR SPECIES: *Sauger* (p. 154): smaller; dorsal fins are lighter with more defined rows of spots; no dark spot on caudal fin and no white spot on lower lobe of caudal fin.

Sauger

large, glassy eyes

dark spot at base of first dorsal fin

white spots on tips of anal and caudal fins

LENGTH: *Average:* 40–60 cm. *Maximum:* 85 cm.
WEIGHT: *Average:* 1–2 kg. *Maximum:* 7 kg.

Size Comparisons

Sometimes it is difficult to conceptualize the actual sizes of fishes without a comparison. The following is a chart of relative sizes of fishes according to two different references. Average lengths are shown for each species.

Small fishes are compared to the Canadian dollar coin (loonie). (Shown at ¼ scale.)

Large fishes are compared to a page in this book. (Shown at ¹⁄₂₀ scale.)

Deepwater Sculpin
Length: Avg: 3–6 cm
Max: 7 cm

Iowa Darter
Length: Avg: 4–5 cm
Max: 6 cm

Northern Redbelly Dace
Length: Avg: 4–5 cm
Max: 7 cm

Ninespine Stickleback
Length: Avg: 5 cm
Max: 7 cm

Brook Stickleback
Length: Avg: 5 cm
Max: 9 cm

Fathead Minnow
Length: Avg: 4–8 cm
Max: 10 cm

Shorthead Sculpin
Length: Avg: 5–7 cm
Max: 11 cm

Slimy Sculpin
Length: Avg: 6 cm
Max: 9 cm

Brassy Minnow
Length: Avg: 5–7.5 cm
Max: 9 cm

River Shiner
Length: Avg: 5–7.5 cm
Max: 11 cm

Emerald Shiner
Length: Avg: 5–7.5 cm
Max: 12 cm

Longnose Dace
Length: Avg: 5–9 cm
Max: 14 cm

Lake Chub
Length: Avg: 5–9 cm
Max: 17 cm

Spottail Shiner
Length: Avg: 6–8 cm
Max: 12 cm

Finescale Dace
Length: Avg: 7 cm
Max: 9 cm

Logperch
Length: Avg: 7–9 cm
Max: 10 cm

Spoonhead Sculpin
Length: Avg: 8 cm
Max: 14 cm

Pygmy Whitefish
Length: Avg: 10 cm
Max: 13 cm

Redside Shiner
Length: Avg: 10 cm
Max: 12 cm

Western Silvery Minnow
Length: Avg: 8–10 cm
Max: 11 cm

Trout-perch
Length: Avg: 7.5–10 cm
Max: 13 cm

Pearl Dace
Length: Avg: 7–10 cm
Max: 17 cm

Stonecat
Length: Avg: 15–20 cm
Max: 25 cm

Mountain Sucker
Length: Avg: 13–17 cm
Max: 22 cm

Largescale Sucker
Length: Avg: 10 cm (juvenile)
Max: 60 cm (adult; British Columbia)

Arctic Lamprey
Length: Avg: 10 cm (ammocoete)
Max: 15 cm (ammocoete)

Flathead Chub
Length: Avg: 20–30 cm
Max: 37 cm

Round Whitefish
Length: Avg: 20–30 cm
Max: 35 cm

Yellow Perch
Length: Avg: 20–25 cm
Max: 39 cm

Brook Trout
Length: Avg: 15–30 cm
Max: 78 cm

Golden Trout
Length: Avg: 15–25 cm
Max: 50 cm

Shortjaw Cisco
Length: Avg: 27–40 cm
Max: 51 cm

Northern Pikeminnow
Length: Avg: 30 cm
Max: 47 cm

Shorthead Redhorse
Length: Avg: 30 cm
Max: 45 cm

Mooneye
Length: Avg: 25–30 cm
Max: 32 cm

Cisco
Length: Avg: 20–30 cm
Max: 45 cm

Cutthroat Trout
Length: Avg: 20–40 cm
Max: 74 cm

Brown Trout
Length: Avg: 25–40 cm
Max: 87 cm

Mountain Whitefish
Length: Avg: 25–45 cm
Max: 63 cm

Arctic Grayling
Length: Avg: 30–40 cm
Max: 55 cm

Goldeye
Length: Avg: 35 cm
Max: 50 cm

Sauger
Length: Avg: 30–45 cm
Max: 66 cm

Rainbow Trout
Length: Avg: 30–45 cm
Max: 81 cm

Longnose Sucker
Length: Avg: 30–50 cm
Max: 55 cm

White Sucker
Length: Avg: 30–50 cm
Max: 58 cm

Quillback
Length: Avg: 40–50 cm
Max: 56 cm

Silver Redhorse
Length: Avg: 40–50 cm
Max: 64 cm

Bull Trout
Length: Avg: 40–50 cm
Max: 85 cm

Northern Pike
Length: Avg: 40–50 cm
Max: 1.2 m

Lake Whitefish
Length: Avg: 40–55 cm
Max: 67 cm

Walleye
Length: Avg: 40–60 cm
Max: 85 cm

Burbot
Length: Avg: 40–60 cm
Max: 1 m

Lake Trout
Length: Avg: 45–65 cm
Max: 1 m

Lake Sturgeon
Length: Avg: 0.75–1 m
Max: 1.7 m

OTHER ALBERTA FISHES

COMMON CARP (JAPANESE KOI) *Cyprinus carpio*

Although abundant and common in parts of neighbouring Montana and Saskatchewan, the introduced and generally despised Common Carp is thankfully neither common nor well established in Alberta. The domesticated variety of this carp, the ornamental Japanese Koi, has been illegally released into several urban ponds in the Edmonton area. Disarmingly pretty to watch, this robust, multi-coloured fish has a bad reputation of out-competing native fishes and destroying shoreline habitat by rooting along the shallow lake and stream bottoms like aquatic pigs.

ID: chunky, large-scaled fish; displays a variety of colour patterns (orange patches and mottled black and white seem common for Alberta specimens); two large, easily visible barbels on upper jaw.

SIZE: *Average length:* 30–60 cm. *Average weight:* 0.5–1.5 kg.

GOLDFISH *Carassius auratus*

This popular aquarium fish periodically shows up in many town ponds in Alberta, but our harsh winters usually prevent it from living more than a couple of years. A small population of Goldfish were released (probably from an aquarium) into Henderson Lake near Lethbridge, and the result is a small community of Goldfish. Because of the presence of Northern Pike and the cold winter months, the Henderson Lake population may be gone. Goldfish have also been illegally released into storm water ponds in Edmonton and St. Albert, as well as Granum Pond and Foremost Reservoir.

ID: all golden or bronzed orange; large caudal fin; rounded body.

SIZE: *Average length:* 5–8 cm. *Maximum length:* 20 cm.

GRASS CARP *Ctenopharyngodon idella*

Originally, the Grass Carp is from China. The genetically engineered creatures found in Alberta, though, are quite different from individuals native to Asia. These Grass Carp are "triploid," meaning that they have 76 chromosomes instead of 48 and therefore have a low probability of reproducing. They were introduced to the irrigation canals of the prairies and to Henderson Lake to keep the vegetation at bay. There have been problems and worries with triploid introductions into irrigation ditches that may be linked to natural waterways. They have been discovered in commercial fisheries in southern reservoirs.

ID: silver white colour; thick-bodied; very large scales; large head; forked caudal fin.

SIZE: *Maximum length:* 50 cm. *Maximum weight:* 2.5 kg.

ARCTIC CHAR *Salvelinus alpinus*

In 2001, an unknown number of Arctic Char escaped from an illegal fish farm near Calgary and leaked into Lott Creek, a tributary of the Elbow River. The Arctic Char's ability to adapt to cold waters could shake loose the last strongholds of one of Alberta's endangered fishes, the Bull Trout. Twenty-seven Arctic Char have been caught in the creek, and biologists are snorkelling the Elbow River with spear guns during spawning season to ensure that spawning areas are kept clear for Bull Trout. It could be a few years before some of the Arctic Char begin spawning, so vigilance will be necessary to continue to keep the local Bull Trout populations safe.

ID: dark background with yellowish, red or bluish spots; white leading edges to bottom fins. *Spawning:* bright red belly.

SIZE: *Average length:* 6–20 cm. *Average weight:* 200–500 g.

DOLLY VARDEN *Salvelinus malma*

These trout are native to western North America and eastern Asia, with mostly anadromous but also some freshwater populations. In 1974, a university researcher obtained a government permit to release his research subjects into Alberta's Chester Lake. The unfortunate researcher had unknowingly received Dolly Varden from a river in the Yukon that was thought to contain Arctic Char. It was an honest mistake, as the northern subspecies of the Dolly Varden can be quite similar to its char relative. The Dolly Varden has been caught in the surrounding tributaries, which indicates its dispersal ability. In Alberta, viewing of Dolly Varden is mainly limited to the shore of Chester Lake in Kananaskis. Go in autumn, when the biting bugs have died down but before the snow flies. It's a lovely alpine lake and the autumn colours of this northern char are at their peak and make the hike worthwhile.

ID: dark body with pinkish belly; red or pink spots; white leading edges to lower fins; dark caudal and dorsal fin. *Spawning male:* develops a kype.

SIZE: *Average length:* 20–30 cm. *Average weight:* 0.5–1.5 kg.

Dolly Varden

WESTERN MOSQUITOFISH *Gambusia affinis*

In addition to having an appetite for mosquito larvae, the Western Mosquitofish is an aggressive and adaptable fish. These last two attributes were apparently unknown to government officials in 1924 when they introduced this popular aquarium fish to the Cave and Basin Marsh in Banff National Park. The motive for the introduction was to spare the bathing tourists from biting bugs. The fish does eat mosquito larvae, but not enough to warrant its destructive presence in the delicate ecology of the marshes. This introduction has occurred around the globe, resulting in the damage of ecosystems and even the extinction of some species. The Western Mosquitofish is one of two livebearing fishes living in Alberta. Parks Canada has built a viewing platform in the marshes so visitors can get a good look at African Jewelfish, Sailfin Molly and Western Mosquitofish, the three alien fish in the marsh.

ID: seemingly swollen "bellies," especially on females; supraterminal mouth; large eyes; thick caudal peduncle; squared caudal fin with rows of dark spots; dorsal fin also has spots. *Female:* anal fin rays are relatively equal; dorsal fin origin is slightly behind origin of anal fin. *Male:* smaller than female; anal fin has increasingly long rays; origin of dorsal fin is far behind origin of anal fin.

SIZE: *Average length:* 2–4 cm. *Maximum length:* 4.4 cm (female); 2.8 cm (male).

SAILFIN MOLLY *Poecilia latipinna*

In 1960, several pairs of black Sailfin Molly were illegally released into the Cave and Basin Marsh in Banff National Park. Despite the unfortunate effects this fish has had on the natural system of the marsh, it has provided an interesting look at both genetics and Darwin's theory of natural selection. By 1988, a large proportion of the population had reverted back to its "wild" appearance, a mottled white-and-black pattern. The larger numbers of this morph indicate that it seems to be better adapted to the environment of the brackish marsh. • Sailfin Molly are native to the southeastern states and the Gulf of Mexico. Populations have been introduced to places such as Hawaii for mosquito control, although Sailfin Molly are mostly herbivorous, eating primarily algae. Sailfin Molly are livebearers—females give birth to live young instead of laying eggs. They can carry up to 60 young. Another alien resident in the marsh, the Western Mosquitofish, is also a livebearer.

ID: small; deep-bodied; most of the population is covered with dark mottling; possible all-black morphs; mouth supraterminal; rounded caudal fin. *Female:* sharp rise to dorsal fin; dorsal fin origin behind pelvic fin origin. *Male:* smaller than female; slight rise to dorsal fin; longer dorsal fin; origin of dorsal fin even with origin of pelvic fins.

SIZE: *Maximum length:* 5 cm (female); 3.3 cm (male).

THREESPINE STICKLEBACK *Gasterosteus aculeatus*

In the 1970s, the Threespine Stickleback was released into Hasse Lake, west of Edmonton, likely making its way to Alberta via a picklejar in the car of a misguided fish-lover who was returning from a vacation in British Columbia. It has also been found in Lake Eden and other storm ponds around Edmonton. This aggressive fish may compete with the Brook Stickleback, a native species, and authorities are considering taking measures to eradicate it.

• The Threespine Stickleback's breeding rituals are similar to those of the other two stickleback species in Alberta. However, female Threespines have a voracious appetite for young of their own species, and sometimes gangs of females will overtake a single guarding male, raiding the nest. Sneakier, immature females will fake the desire to mate with a male. Thinking he is getting another mate, the male will let her enter the nest, naively thinking she is spawning while she is actually munching on his prized eggs. The fascinating spawning and courtship behaviour of this exotic little fish can easily be observed by shoreline fishwatchers. Find a calm piece of water, put on your polarized sunglasses and simply watch along the margins of weedy or brush-filled shallows. These fish will let cautious observers approach to within a couple of metres. Peering down an ice-fishing hole is also a good way to see these fascinating fish, but you may need to attract them by dropping a bit of bait down the hole. Tiny bits of bread crumbs or hard-boiled eggs are excellent.

ID: large eyes; thin caudal peduncle; two large spines on back, one small spine in front of dorsal fin; small spine before anal fin, large spine near pectoral fin; plates in pectoral area; squared caudal fin.

SIZE: *Average length:* 4–7 cm. *Maximum length:* 10 cm.

PRICKLY SCULPIN *Cottus asper*

In 1989, one specimen may have travelled awry down the Peace River. Fish biologists are still keeping a close eye out to see if there is a spawning population in the Albertan leg of the Peace River or in one of its tributaries.

ID: long anal fin with 15–19 rays; anal fin length is longer than head length; dark barring on fins; dark spot on posterior end of first dorsal fin; one pore at the tip of "chin"; "prickly" on back and sides.

SIZE: *Maximum length:* 15 cm.

SMALLMOUTH BASS *Micropterus dolomieu*

Beginning in 1977, Smallmouth Bass were introduced into Island Lake north of Smoky Lake for recreational purposes. These fish put up a serious fight on the end of a hook and are constantly being requested for stocking by homesick, transplanted eastern Canadians. Other proposed introductions have been quashed because of worries about introducing a predator that could escape to larger water bodies such as the North Saskatchewan River. There is a small population in Island Lake, but the population is not managed. If this population disappears it will not be restocked.

ID: light coloured with black mottling; two dorsal fins are joined by a membrane; relatively large mouth.

SIZE: *Average length:* 30 cm. *Average weight:* 0.5–1.5 kg.

Smallmouth Bass, Largemouth Bass, Atlantic Salmon, Coho Salmon, Kokanee (land-locked Sockeye salmon) and Arctic Char were stocked in a number of water bodies in earlier days of fisheries management. Thankfully, most of these introductions have been unsuccessful. However, expansion in aquaculture (fish farming) in Alberta more recently has seen many exotic species being imported, with the inevitable escapees becoming unwanted introductions (such as Arctic Char in the Bow River and Grass Carp in southern reservoirs).

AFRICAN JEWELFISH *Hemichromis bimaculatus*

A popular aquarium fish, the African Jewelfish is an unwanted but beautiful addition to the Cave and Basin Marsh in Banff National Park. Introduced from an illegal aquarium release, the African Jewelfish is a highly territorial species from central and northern Africa. Spawning Jewelfish will pair off, wrestling, locking jaws and testing each other's worth as mate and protector of the nest. These fish are so aggressive that they must be the only two fish in an aquarium when spawning lest they tear the other inhabitants apart. • The introduction of this species allowed biologists to examine the consequences of introducing such an exotic species to the area. The native resident fish in the marsh, the Banff subspecies of the Longnose Dace, is now extinct.

ID: rounded body with thick caudal peduncle; rounded caudal fin; large eyes; terminal mouth; long dorsal fin; body is green and red with mostly blue spots along entire body including head and fins; three black spots: one on the operculum, one on the middle of the body and one at the end of the caudal peduncle. *Spawning:* both sexes turn bright red, all spots remain.

SIZE: *Average length:* 5–8 cm.

GLOSSARY

abundant: seen regularly in large numbers.

alkali: containing sodium (salt).

anadromous: a fish that hatches in fresh water, lives its adult life in salt water and returns to fresh water to spawn.

at risk: any species that is considered threatened or endangered by the Government of Alberta.

back eddy: a vortex or "whirlpool" caused by an interruption in the flow of water (usually caused by an obstruction).

benthic: pertaining to the bottom of a lake or a river (see diagram on page 19).

broadcast spawner: a species of fish that releases eggs and milt into the water without providing a nest or parental care; this type of spawning is usually associated with synchronized breeding of a large group of fish.

collapsed population: a population that has fallen below the number of individuals it would need to consistently produce abundant young (also known as recruitment overfishing).

common: seen regularly in small numbers.

deep body: refers to the longer than average height of a fish from back to belly.

detritus: dead and decaying organic matter.

drainage basin: an area of lakes, streams and watersheds that drains into a specific river, lake or ocean.

extirpated: a species that is extinct from a certain area but is still present in the world.

filter-feeder: an aquatic animal that traps and removes food particles from flowing water; in Alberta, fishes often filter-feed using their gill rakers.

ichthyologist: a person who studies fishes.

keeled: refers to the curved, sharp-edged shape of the body or fins of some species.

larva: a developmental stage of many animals, including insects and fishes, that occurs between hatching and adulthood.

laterally compressed: "skinny"; refers to a body that is thin from side to side.

locally: when a certain species is only found in specific areas.

may be at risk: a species that may be at risk of extinction or becoming threatened but has not yet received a detailed risk assessment.

main stem: the usually large, main arm of a river into which all related tributaries flow.

milt: fish sperm, released by males during spawning.

papillae: small, fleshy projections from the skin.

pelagic: refers to the open water in a water body (see diagram on page 19).

piscivorous: an animal that feeds exclusively on fishes.

plankton: microscopic living plant or animal matter that is moved passively by water currents; plant matter is called "phytoplankton," animal matter is referred to as "zooplankton," and bacterial matter is called "bacterioplankton."

rare: seen only once or twice during the year.

redd: a nest of fish eggs dug into a riverbed (usually gravel or sand).

refugia: areas that have not been altered by extreme changes in climate such as glaciation.

salmonid: a member of the family Salmonidae, which is composed of all whitefishes, graylings, chars, trouts and salmons.

Scheckstoff: an alarm substance that is released when the skin cells of a small fish (usually a schooling fish, such as a minnow) are broken.

secure: a species whose population is not in danger of extinction, extirpation or becoming at risk.

sensitive: any species that is not at risk of extinction but may require special attention or protection to prevent it from becoming at risk.

silt: soil particles smaller than sand and larger than clay.

spawning: the act of fish reproduction; the external mixing of the milt of a male fish and the eggs of a female fish.

stocking: the human introduction of fishes to a water body, mostly for the purpose of recreational fishing.

striated: marked with parallel lines.

subspecies: a distinct population of a species that occupies a particular geographic area or habitat and is capable of interbreeding with other populations of the same species.

summerkill: a die off of fishes owing to oxygen depletion occuring in warm weather; warm water encourages algae blooms, and the decomposition of the algae depletes oxygen needed by fishes.

tapetum lucidum: a reflective membrane at the back of the eye that reflects back to the rods and cones whatever light they didn't first catch. Essentially, this membrane gives the retina a second chance at reflecting light and is an adaptation to seeing in low-light levels. It is what makes nocturnal animals' eyes glow yellow or green in the dark.

tributary: a flowing water body that feeds into another water body, usually a larger stream, river or lake.

tubercle: a fleshy nodule that can occur on the skin or fins; prominent mostly on breeding males of some species.

turbidity: the measurement of the amount of silt or loose organic material in a water body; the more turbid a water body is, the more difficult it is to see through.

uncommon: seen on a few occasions (more than twice) during the year.

undetermined status: any species for which insufficient information, knowledge or data is available to reliably evaluate its status.

winterkill: a die off of fishes owing to the lack of oxygen under the ice; the ice forms a barrier between the water body and the atmosphere, so there is no source of fresh oxygen until the ice breaks up in the spring. Decaying plants and algae under the ice often deplete the oxygen supply to critical levels for fishes in most shallow Alberta lakes (and some rivers).

CHECKLIST

The following checklist contains 65 fishes that have been recorded in Alberta. Species are grouped by family and listed in taxonomic order. A (+) indicates an introduced species. In addition, the following status categories from The General Status of Alberta Wild Species 2000 are noted: sensitive or at risk (se) or may be at risk (mar). If the species name is in italics, it is found in the Appendix species (p. 158).

LAMPREYS
(Petromyzontidae)
- ❏ Arctic Lamprey

STURGEONS
(Acipenseridae)
- ❏ Lake Sturgeon

MOONEYES
(Hiodontidae)
- ❏ Goldeye
- ❏ Mooneye

MINNOWS (Cyprinidae)
- ❏ Common Carp +
- ❏ Goldfish +
- ❏ Grass Carp +
- ❏ Lake Chub
- ❏ Western Silvery Minnow (mar)
- ❏ Brassy Minnow
- ❏ Pearl Dace
- ❏ Emerald Shiner
- ❏ River Shiner
- ❏ Spottail Shiner
- ❏ Northern Redbelly Dace
- ❏ Finescale Dace (se)
- ❏ Fathead Minnow
- ❏ Flathead Chub
- ❏ Northern Pikeminnow (se)
- ❏ Longnose Dace
- ❏ Redside Shiner

SUCKERS
(Catostomidae)
- ❏ Quillback
- ❏ Longnose Sucker
- ❏ White Sucker
- ❏ Largescale Sucker
- ❏ Mountain Sucker
- ❏ Silver Redhorse
- ❏ Shorthead Redhorse

BULLHEAD CATFISHES
(Ictaluridae)
- ❏ Stonecat

PIKES (Esocidae)
- ❏ Northern Pike

TROUTS (Salmonidae)
- ❏ Cisco
- ❏ Shortjaw Cisco (mar)
- ❏ Lake Whitefish
- ❏ Pygmy Whitefish (mar)
- ❏ Round Whitefish
- ❏ Mountain Whitefish
- ❏ Arctic Grayling (se)
- ❏ Cutthroat Trout
- ❏ Rainbow Trout + (native populations mar)
- ❏ Golden Trout +
- ❏ Brown Trout +
- ❏ Arctic Char +
- ❏ Bull Trout (se)
- ❏ Dolly Varden +
- ❏ Brook Trout +
- ❏ Lake Trout (se)

TROUT-PERCHES
(Percopsidae)
- ❏ Trout-perch

CODS (Gadidae)
- ❏ Burbot

LIVEBEARERS
(Poeciliidae)
- ❏ Western Mosquitofish +
- ❏ Sailfin Molly +

STICKLEBACKS
(Gasterosteidae)
- ❏ Brook Stickleback
- ❏ Ninespine Stickleback
- ❏ Threespine Stickleback +

SCULPINS (Cottidae)
- ❏ Prickly Sculpin
- ❏ Slimy Sculpin
- ❏ Shorthead Sculpin (mar)
- ❏ Spoonhead Sculpin (mar)
- ❏ Deepwater Sculpin

SUNFISHES
(Centrarchidae)
- ❏ Smallmouth Bass +

PERCHES (Percidae)
- ❏ Iowa Darter
- ❏ Logperch
- ❏ Yellow Perch
- ❏ Sauger (se)
- ❏ Walleye

CICHLIDS (Cichlidae)
- ❏ African Jewelfish +

Selected References

Behnke, R.J. 2002. *Trout and Salmon of North America.* The Free Press, New York.

Boschung, H.T., Jr., J.D. Williams et al. 1983. *National Audubon Society Field Guide to North American Fishes, Whales and Dolphins.* Alfred A. Knopf, New York.

Coad, B.W., H. Waszczuk et al. 1995. *The Encyclopedia of Canadian Fishes.* Canadian Museum of Nature and Canadian Sportfishing Productions, Singapore.

Helfman, G.S., B.B. Collette et al. 1997. *The Diversity of Fishes.* Blackwell Science, Malden, Massachusetts.

McClane, A.J. 1974. *McClane's New Standard Fishing Encyclopedia and International Angling Guide.* Holt, Rinehart and Winston, USA.

McPhail, J.D., C.C. Lindsey. 1970. *Freshwater Fish of Northwestern Canada and Alaska.* Bulletin 173. Fisheries Research Board of Canada, Ottawa, Ontario.

Nelson, J.S., M.J. Paetz. 1992. *The Fishes of Alberta.* The University of Alberta Press, Edmonton, Alberta.

Nelson, J.S. 1994. *Fishes of the World.* 3rd ed. John Wiley and Sons, New York.

Nelson, J.S. (chairman), E.J. Crossman, H. Espinosa-Péres, L.T. Findley, C.R. Gilbert, R.N. Lea and J.D. Williams. 2003 manuscript. *Common and Scientific Names of Fishes From the United States, Canada and Mexico.* 6th ed. Special Publication, American Fisheries Society, Bethesda, Maryland.

Schultz, K. 2000. *Ken Schultz's Fishing Encyclopedia.* IDG Books Worldwide, Foster City, California.

Scott, W.B., E.J. Crossman. 1998. *Freshwater Fishes of Canada.* Galt House Publications, Oakville, Ontario.

FURTHER INFORMATION

Alberta Conservation Association
P.O. Box 40027
Baker Centre Post Office
Edmonton, Alberta T5J 4M9
Phone: (780) 427-5192
http://www.ab-conservation.com/

Alberta Fish and Game Association
6924 – 104 Street
Edmonton, Alberta T6H 2L7
Phone: (780) 437-2342
http://www.afga.org

Canada's Aquatic Environments: Fish
http://www.aquatic.uoguelph.ca/fish/fish.htm

Edmonton Trout Fishing Club: The Virtual Flycaster
http://www.freenet.edmonton.ab.ca/edmtrout/index.html

FishBase: A Global Information System on Fishes
This site includes a fishwatcher link!
http://www.fishbase.org/home.htm

Government of Alberta: Sustainable Resource Development
At the second site listed, click on "Fish Identification" and take the fish quiz.
http://www3.gov.ab.ca/srd/fw/fish/index.html
http://www3.gov.ab.ca/srd/fw/fishing/index.html

Ichthyology Web Resources
http://www2.biology.ualberta.ca/jackson.hp/
IWR/index.php

North American Native Fishes Association
http://www.nanfa.org/

Royal Alberta Museum
12845 – 102 Avenue
Edmonton, Alberta T5N 0M6
Phone: (780) 453-9100
http://www.royalalbertamuseum.ca/

Trout Unlimited Canada: Alberta Council
P.O. Box 6270, Station D
Calgary, Alberta T2P 2C8
Phone: (403) 221-8360
http://www.tucanada.org/alberta/index.htm

INDEX OF SCIENTIFIC NAMES

This index references only the primary species accounts.

INDEX OF COMMON NAMES

ABOUT THE AUTHORS

AMANDA JOYNT

Still in the early days of her professional life as an ecologist, Amanda Joynt has already enjoyed a varied career. Originally from the Okanagan Valley of British Columbia, she received her B.Sc. in Environmental and Conservation Science from the University of Alberta. She has banded burrowing owls in southern Alberta, guided tours for the Tofield Snow Goose Festival, mapped vegetation in Tuktut Nogait National Park in the Canadian Arctic and surveyed rare plants in the Black Hills of South Dakota. She also initiated an environmental learning program that encourages Tanzanian and Canadian students to compare their environmental situations and knowledge. Amanda now enjoys sharing her enthusiasm for animals and plants as a nature writer. In her spare time, she is a volunteer dog-walker at the Edmonton SPCA.

MICHAEL G. SULLIVAN

The provincial fisheries science specialist for Alberta Environment, Michael Sullivan is also a consultant to federal and provincial governments about methods of fisheries management and ways of protecting aquatic ecosystems. He has done extensive research into the causes of fish stock depletion and has designed effective management strategies for maintaining fish populations, which have been adopted in British Columbia, Ontario and Wisconsin. Michael's research has sometimes kept him in the field year-round, and he is as contented mushing a dog team in the frozen North as he is canoeing down a river. An award-winning athlete in the biathlon, he is an all-round outdoorsman who also enjoys scuba diving, fishing, hunting, birdwatching and ice climbing.

THE ILLUSTRATOR: IAN SHELDON

Ian Sheldon is a Canadian-born artist who has lived in South Africa, Singapore and England, and has travelled much of the world. Following his Masters of Science degree at the University of Alberta, Ian decided to devote his attention to the fine arts. He has many natural history books under his belt as both writer and illustrator, including Lone Pine's *Bugs of Alberta*.